SPIRITUAL WARRIOR IV

Conquering the Enemies of the Mind

B.T. SWAMI

With Love

B. T. Swami

HARI
NAMA
PRESS

Hari-Nama Press gratefully acknowledges the BBT for the use of verses and purports from Srila Prabhupada's books. All such verses and purports are © Bhaktivedanta Book Trust International, Inc.

The publisher gratefully acknowledges the kind permission of Goloka Books in allowing us the use of their artwork for incorporation into our cover design.

First printing 2004

Cover and interior design by Subala dasa / Ecstatic Creations
Cover artwork by Philip Malpass / Goloka Books

Printed in the United States of America

ISBN softbound: 1-885414-16-1

Library of Congress Control Number: 2003116084

Persons interested in the subject matter of this book are invited to correspond with the publisher:

Hari-Nama Press
PO Box 76451, Capitol Hill, Washington, DC 20013

www.ifast.net/hnp

SPIRITUAL WARRIOR IV

Conquering the Enemies of the Mind

Dedication
I dedicate this book to the millions of people around the world who are struggling with chronic depression. May this book aid you in a speedy recovery.

Contents

Do Not Fear • Anxiety Minimizes the Lord's Supremacy •
Introspection • What is Anxiety • How to Avoid Anxiety •
Do Not Fear the Future • Plan for the Worst, Expect
the Best • Remember the Consequences • Collect the
Facts and Then Act • Keep the Mind Busy • Avoid the
Trifles • Help and Serve Other People • Understand the
Influence of Karma • Establish a Worry Time • Looking
into the Scriptures • Blazing Fire of Anxiety • Anxiety for
the Welfare of Others • The Spiritual World is Without
Anxiety • The Material Disease • A Saintly Person Does
Not Cause Anxiety • Surrender to God Dissipates All
Anxieties • Exemplary Personalities • Service to God •
Questions and Answers

Acknowledgements

I would sincerely like to thank Lauren Kossis for the initial editing of the book. I would also like to thank Jambavan Dasa for Sanskrit editing and Jason Gerick and Lisa Webb for proofreading. I would like to thank all of my disciples who transcribed the many audiotapes, and Adam Kenney, Krista Helfer, and Stewart Cannon for the layout, final editing, and all things necessary to bring this book to press. I would also like to thank the following people from the United Kingdom for financing the printing of *Spiritual Warrior IV* and *V*—Kamlesh Gandhi, Jean Williams, Eddie Anobah, Citi-sakti Dasi. You are wonderful spiritual warriors, who are eager to assist others in conquering the enemies of the mind in order to make the mind the best friend.

Foreword

In the midst of numerous self-help books decorating libraries and bookstore shelves, it gives me immense pleasure to welcome His Holiness Bhakti Tirtha Swami's *Spiritual Warrior IV: Conquering the Enemies of the Mind.* Why? Simply because this will provide readers with real glimpses of unique technologies to deal with depression, anxiety, anger, and grief. It is heart warming to note that the author does not demean the biological aspect of these diseases but provides a compendium for persons who are getting or seeking help with biological therapies. As it is very evident from the author's preface, *Spiritual Warrior IV* and *V* will offer readers different spiritual technologies for accomplishing this purpose.

This very well written book provides an approach encompassing not only material but also spiritual paradigms incorporating all of the complexities life has to offer. At the same time, B.T. Swami accomplishes this without proselytizing us to follow his chosen spiritual path. However, he never denies or sugar coats his commitment to his Vaisnava tradition as we find in authors of other self-help books who try to portray themselves as secular.

Now let us examine this book chapter by chapter. In the first chapter, Avoiding Excessive Anxiety, the author invites us to be introspective which is also highly essential to biological psychiatry. Hence persons seeking help for anxiety who do not introspect will never achieve remission. B.T. Swami further defines anxiety and gives the process for avoiding its devastating effects. He also answers us on the basis of scriptures that "the Supreme Lord has the duty to protect and fulfill his promises." To support this, he has extensively quoted great personalities of the Vedic tradition.

The second chapter invites us to choose love over fear. B.T. Swami gives a "clarion call for spiritual warfare" and points out that, "unless people take tremendous shelter of the spiritual culture," fear will prevail. And he correctly points out, "love cannot develop in the presence of fear." He goes on to describe different kinds of fear and then analyzes them with his spiritual vision. He warns us not to be victims of "the culture of fear" otherwise "we will overly absorb ourselves in eating, sleeping, mating, and fearing." The author calls upon "spiritual warriors" to recognize those who are emotionally shut down and help them become transcendentally alive.

The next chapter deals with managing anger. The author opens this chapter with caution to spiritual seekers that if they don't employ introspection, they may fall back to their past bad habits. Further, he calls upon spiritual warriors "to recognize our consciousness to be the battlefield and our weapons to be genuine knowledge, integrity, compassion, and love." This follows with an analysis of anger as well as its causes and myths.

B.T. Swami very profoundly discusses triggers of anger, the five shoulds, and the four blamers—a practical workbook to help readers. He of course does not leave us in limbo but gives "nine positive ways to deal with shoulds and blamers." He reminds us, as mental health professionals, that there is healthy as well as unhealthy anger.

Apart from healthy anger, the author next introduces us to healthy grieving. To facilitate proper understanding of grief, he has categorized it with eight stages ranging from denial, anger, guilt, fear, pain, sorrow, acceptance, and finally returning to pursuits of love. B.T. Swami tells us that to grieve in a healthy manner, we should be able to "name it, face it, feel it, and release it in order to genuinely let go and move away from the experience." Insightfully, he reveals to us the real cause of grief—our separation from the Supreme Lord.

The author then tackles the problem of depression, which can sometimes fall into the category of the dark night of the soul. This chapter has been profoundly written. The author analyzes the causes of depression, the types including biological factors, and provides us with technologies of how to cope with depression in healthy ways. To accomplish this goal, he invites us to develop the consciousness to consistently thank the Supreme in any situation. To develop such consciousness, he tells us briefly how to inculcate such ability. Further, he gives step-by-step directions how to cope with depression, panic attacks, and also how to help children who have become victims of depression.

Addiction and the process of recovery increase our awareness of what some call a spiritual emergency or a spiritual crisis that many choose to label as nothing more than a mental disorder. Furthermore, B.T. Swami delves into the Twelve Steps, which help us understand the various stages that an addict must pass through on the path to recovery. Finally, he compares the aspiring spiritualist to a recovering addict due to the many attachments and temptations that continue to enslave the person.

The last chapter of this book is a welcome relief—laughter good for the body and soul. B.T. Swami invites us to accelerate the joy. He discusses laughter as therapy and elucidates physical and psychological benefits of laughter. The author further enriches this chapter by providing reflections from his own life and supports his points by quoting from ancient scriptures. Finally, he beautifully sums up the root cause of psychological disorders by helping us to realize "we have created them. We have hosted them so now we can laugh as we reject their existences and as we see them as perverted reflections and indications of true emotions connected with the Godhead."

Let us welcome this unique book into the armamentarium of the mental health arena and learn from an **acarya** (teacher who leads by example). Lastly, I am sure those readers who are not yet spiritual warriors will surely like to join B.T. Swami and become one.

Ravi P. Singh, M.D., M.P.H.
Diplomat, American Board of
Psychiatry and Neurology

Editor's Preface

The *Spiritual Warrior* series consists of lectures given by His Holiness Bhakti Tirtha Swami (Swami Krishnapada) to a wide variety of live radio and television audiences around the world, over a period of several years. Since the topics were originally presented in spoken form, the style is conversational and informal. In the editing process, we have modified the text to enhance readability, yet sought to preserve some of the verbal nuances and maintain the mood of the original presentations. By so doing, we hope to create an atmosphere that literally makes you part of the audience so that you can experience the powerful presence of the speaker as he shares essential nourishment for the soul.

We would like to mention several other stylistic considerations. In the course of his discussions, B.T. Swami includes perspectives from many different spiritual philosophies; however, because his audiences are composed mainly of people in

7

the Christian and Vedic traditions, he makes the most extensive references to these scriptures. At times, he uses Sanskrit terminology from the Vedas, a vast body of ancient scriptures originating from the area of the world known today as India. We have endeavored to keep many of these terms and have tried to explain them within the context of the discussion. When coming upon such terms, if one needs additional information and clarification, we invite you to consult the glossary. However, there are some terms we would like to initially clarify:

- When His Holiness B.T. Swami refers to the one God that we all know of, he uses different terminologies. Sometimes he says the Supreme Lord, the Supreme Personality of Godhead, Mother-Father God, or Krishna.

- He often uses the word "devotees." He is drawing attention to those spiritualists who are connected to the Vedic tradition as well as to all aspiring spiritualists who are embarking on the spiritual journey.

- He also uses the term "nine-fold process", which refers to various activities that a person engages in during his or her spiritual practices of devotion to God, such as hearing about the Lord, speaking about Him, remembering Him, praying to Him, serving Him, fully surrendering, and so on.

Furthermore, the end of each chapter includes many of the questions and answers exchanged during the original lectures. We hope that these will respond to some of the concerns that arise during the course of your reading. These discussions between Bhakti Tirtha Swami and the audience may also give you different angles from which to view the topics presented.

This book is the fourth volume in our *Spiritual Warrior* series. The first three volumes, *Spiritual Warrior I: Uncovering Spiritual Truths in Psychic Phenomena*, *Spiritual Warrior II: Transforming Lust into Love*, and *Spiritual Warrior III: Solace for the Heart in Difficult Times*, are already in print and have been translated into several languages, along with His Holiness' other works. The information presented in these pages is extremely rare, and we hope you will make the most of the knowledge they contain. If you take these teachings seriously, they can transform your life into a most sublime, loving adventure.

Author's Preface

Spiritual Warrior IV: Conquering the Enemies of the Mind and *Spiritual Warrior V: Making the Mind Your Best Friend* were written at the same time. They are distinct books that stand on their own, but if read together, they compliment each other even more than the previous books in this series.

About fifty-five percent of my ministry is in connection with my own Vaisnava (those who worship a personal God and are connected with what many refer to as the Hindu faith) communities and institutions around the world. The other forty-five percent of my work and teaching is in connection with the international business, medical, and interfaith communities. My special area of interest involves helping leaders to be more authentic, and helping spiritualists of all faiths to rise above stagnations and blocks in order to more truly help themselves and their communities.

After recently finishing a forty-country world teaching tour in which I addressed many of the issues in *Spiritual Warrior IV* and *Spiritual Warrior V*, I wanted to make some of this material available in simple written form to help people overcome their *anarthas*, obstacles, blocks, and stagnations. I saw that, in all of these communities, people were getting stuck and were often experiencing intense mental suffering. As I have been praying to be more of a "global change agent" in assisting people with their suffering, *Spiritual Warrior IV* and *V* are offered in this spirit.

In Sanskrit, we call the main enemies of the mind *bhaya* (fear), *kama* (lust), *krodha* (anger), *lobha* (greed), *matsarya* (envy), *mada* (madness), and *moha* (illusion). Some of their affiliates are grief, depression, chronic anxiety, panic attacks, obsessive compulsive behavior, posttraumatic stress, and phobias. In *Spiritual Warrior IV* and *V*, I address and expose these enemies, and show ways to overcome their influences. Their existence is engendered by the false ego, which means that transforming the false ego into pure ego is the ultimate solution. *Spiritual Warrior IV* and *V* will offer the reader different spiritual technologies for accomplishing this. Once again, spiritual warriors, here is more spiritual ammunition for you in the war of waging peace and love.

Chapter 1

Avoiding Excessive Anxiety

ahankara-krtam bandham
atmano 'rtha-viparyayam
vidvan nirvidya samsara-
cintam turye sthitas tyajet

The false ego of the living entity places
him in bondage and awards him exactly
the opposite of what he really desires.
Therefore, an intelligent person should
give up his constant anxiety to enjoy
material life and remain situated in the
Lord, who is beyond the functions of
material consciousness.

Srimad-Bhagavatam 11.13.29

Do Not Fear

In the ancient Vedic scripture known as the *Bhagavad-gita*, the Lord tells Arjuna:

> *sarva-dharman parityajya*
> *mam ekam saranam vraja*
> *aham tvam sarva-papebhyo*
> *moksayisyami ma sucah*

> Abandon all varieties of religion and just surrender unto Me. I shall deliver you from all sinful reactions. Do not fear.
> *Bhagavad-gita 18.66*

As the Lord ends His conversation with Arjuna in the *Bhagavad-gita*, He tells His servant not to fear or worry, an important instruction for us all. Why does He tell Arjuna to fearlessly abandon all varieties of religion and simply surrender? After describing the processes of *karma-yoga*, *hatha-yoga*, *jnana-yoga*, and *astanga-yoga*, the Lord basically tells Arjuna that such activities are merely prerequisites. As Arjuna ponders this knowledge, Krishna tells him to embrace the essence and abandon the superficial secondary considerations. Accepting the Lord to be our real well-wisher, our great friend, and our ultimate protector is very profound and is the essence of spiritual life. If we could just accept these facts, our worries would not have a substantial foundation to grow.

Among the activities of eating, sleeping, mating, and fearing, the *Srimad-Bhagavatam*, a more advanced Vedic text, describes fear as the most difficult to overcome or conquer because of its presence in all of these other engagements. Anxiety actually inhibits the positive development of love and devotion. Anxiety and fear are attributes that cannot directly coincide with love or devotion. Fear and love go ill together. All activities can fit into one of two categories: *kama* (lust) and *prema* (love). Therefore, a devoted spiritualist needs to become doubtless and fearless. How does a devotee on the spiritual journey acquire these qualities and what interferes with their development? We hope to answer these questions by examining anxiety from psychological, social, and also spiritual perspectives. The true spiritual warrior can never be captured by excessive anxiety because of his or her constant absorption in giving and receiving love.

Anxiety Minimizes the Lord's Supremacy

As we delve deeper into this discussion and examine our great *acaryas*, or spiritual teachers and prophets, we will find that they never took shelter of excessive worry, which hinders the development of the devotional creeper and prevents a person from taking full shelter of God. Excessive worrying indicates that we have lost control of our minds. It means that we have not fully accepted God's love and omniscience in His ultimate position as *krsnas tu bhagavan svayam* or as the Supreme Personality of Godhead who is in control.

In other words, worrying means that a person has failed to appreciate God's position as the possessor of all six opulences (beauty, strength, knowledge, fame, wealth, and renunciation) in full. The person will consequently think of the Lord as unmerciful and will remain overly concerned about their personal fate. Such anxious people will begin to see themselves as the controllers and will doubt the Lord's full presence in their heart. Anxiety minimizes our access to the Lord's constant help and guidance from generation to generation and age to age. Worrying literally minimizes our access to the potency of God in His different *avataras* or incarnations who come to annihilate the miscreants, establish pure devotional service, and protect His devotees.

The Lord tells us to give up such anxiety and He also tells us that we should engage the mind in positive activities:

man-mana bhava mad-bhakto
mad-yaji mam namaskuru
mam evaisyasi yuktvaivam
atmanam mat-parayanah

Engage your mind always in thinking of Me, become My devotee, offer obeisances to Me and worship Me. Being completely absorbed in Me, surely you will come to Me.
Bhagavad-gita 9.34

He tells us not to worry about the outcome. We might compare this verse to the previous verse in *Bhagavad-gita* (18.66) in which the Lord tells Arjuna not to hesitate or fear. Instead of worrying, he should just surrender, and according to that level of surrender, he will receive reciprocation. Next time you find yourself in a state of complete anxiety, consider these factors and allow them to remind you that such worry actually minimizes God's position as the ultimate controller and our well-wisher. It actually denies these facts and takes the place of higher devotion and love.

Introspection

We should use this opportunity to look at our mind in order to harness it and place it more in the service of the Lord. First, we should look at ourselves to determine the extent that excessive worry permeates our lives. This examination will tell us about our level of faith. A *sadhu* or saintly person is supposed to be *drdha-vratah*, or faithful with firm determination and *dhira*, or very grave and focused. What does this tell us about our own mindset?

By engaging in deep introspection, many people will discover that worries and anxieties thoroughly permeate their day-to-day activities. Such anxieties often revolve around physical and economic problems or stem from all types of insignificant matters. For instance, people meditate on what to wear, where to go over the weekend, what to do after they choose a place, and what other people think of them. Such excessive anxieties are solely on the bodily platform and revolve around the individual as the center of the universe. Too much worrying puts an excessive amount of emphasis on our bodies and on matter. A devotee should not remain in this mood. The Supreme Lord makes very strong propositions by telling us not to hesitate, fear, or worry. In spite of the constant assaults against us in the material energy, He tells us to give up our fears and anxieties.

We will offer four different categories with which to broaden our analysis. We will define worry, offer practical techniques to help us address the problem, look closer at certain scriptural references relating to this topic, and finally, hear about the characteristics of some of the outstanding personalities in the scriptures who did not engage in excessive worrying.

What is Anxiety

We can define worry in the following ways:
1. Worry is **a choice** and is often **a way to avoid change**. We sometimes take shelter of worry because it helps us feel busy and allows us to rationalize our lack of concrete action. Instead of taking the proper action, we accept the illusion of activity that anxiety produces.

2. Worry is also **a poor substitute for proper loving action**. It is an artificial activity that we use to minimize the proper and beneficial action. As a result, we just worry. Since we spend so much time worrying, we have less time to actively glorify the Lord. If we place all of our mental and physical energy into worrying, we will not have a sufficient amount left to repose in God.

3. Excessive worry basically deals with **a feeling of powerlessness**. *Sadhus* or saints should not be arrogant or egocentric but very humble. Although they recognize their own lack of power, they understand that the Lord has the ability to accomplish all tasks. Consequently, by letting the power or *sakti* of the Lord work through them, they have access to great power. Actually, excessive anxiety disempowers us and prevents us from allowing God's power to work through us because we have blocked the *sakti*.

4. Worrying is **a way to rehearse dreadful outcomes**. In other words, it creates some of the same effects or feelings that would result from the negative outcome itself. If we analyze the results closely, worry leads to the exact

outcome that we most want to avoid. Since you have practically lived the trauma or misfortune in the mind, you may even experience some of the negative effects. If you continue to meditate on this *mantra*, not only will you mentally experience the situation, you may even turn it into a physical experience.

5. Abandoning worry, *ma sucah*, **does not mean that we stop planning**. We should not give up our concern when we see an improper action; rather, we should plan, think powerfully, and then do the necessary. What do you do if you discover a fire in your house? You immediately leave. You would not just sit on the couch and worry. Obviously, there is a problem, but it is also a time for practical action.

How to Avoid Anxiety

How do we break this pattern of constantly worrying? How can people who have the protection of the greatest shelter still worry so much? Although we can endlessly worry and consider ourselves to be at the mercy of circumstance, we understand the influence of *karma*, which refers to any material action that brings a reaction, binding us to this material world. We also understand that higher authorities, the *devas* (the angelic host) and the Supreme Lord, have control over all things. To the extent that we genuinely surrender, Krishna has the duty to protect and fulfill His part.

Considering these factors, where does all the worry stem from? Does it mean that we think of the Lord as a liar or a cheater who wants to see us in constant fear and to use us in unhealthy ways in His position as an autocrat? Does it mean that we only think of God as the controller who wants to keep us in the material prison? If we consider the sweetness of the Divine Couple or Mother-Father God and we consider how the Lord monitors every action and thought, our level of anxiety should never escalate to such an extent that we do not feel backed or protected when we act righteously. We should never think that God has left us alone without any help or guidance and without any way to get us out of our *maya* or our problems.

We want to find ways to break the worry habits before they break us. If we do not stop such habits, our fears can easily overwhelm us and even turn into chronic depression, phobias, panic attacks, compulsive behaviors, and even suicide. We have all seen people who worry about every little detail. If we simply present them with an idea, they will immediately try to show its fallibility. They have an insecurity complex along with an existential mood about life. They feel defeated before they even start. Such people may even pull out memories from the past and then present these past failures as evidence, but they will not plan or depend on God. Since they will not take the risk, they lead a life of great boredom, frustration, and mediocrity, which also means less *ruci* or spiritual taste. We do not want to fall into these destructive patterns; therefore, we want to offer the following techniques to help rescue our consciousness from such a negative mentality.

Do Not Fear the Future

We should try to avoid any worry that revolves around fears of the future. As we live each day, we should simply do our very best today and let the future take care of itself. When we worry too excessively about the future, we often fail to take the necessary actions that will lead to an auspicious future. In many ways, the future is an extension of the present along with influences from the past. Unfortunately, we can turn into our own greatest enemy. Our own mind can create the exact situations we wish to avoid, and an unhealthy mental culture often blocks the divine power that can work through us. When we worry about the future, we do not offer our best today.

Plan for the Worst, Expect the Best

When we encounter a worry, we should ask ourselves, "What is the worst that could possibly happen?" People sometimes say, "Plan for the worst but expect the best." If we develop this mindset, a setback will not cause such a drastic imbalance because of our backup plan; therefore, we will have a chance to act positively while recognizing God's position as the ultimate controller. By mentally preparing ourselves for the worst, we can calmly improve on a seemingly negative situation since we have already agreed to mentally accept the circumstances.

Remember the Consequences

As we endeavor to avoid worry, we should remind ourselves of the dangers of excessive anxiety in terms of its effects on the body and mind. Some of these consequences include poor relationships, hypertension, depression, physical sickness, boredom, lack of creativity, and a lack of productive activity. The list goes on and on. If we look at the downside and understand the amount of loss that results from anxiety, we may then decide to be gainers instead of losers.

Collect the Facts and Then Act

We should get all of the facts. People often try to make decisions before they have a sufficient amount of information about the problem or issue. This lack of knowledge will definitely result in anxiety. We should look at the entire issue and then develop a plan. We should not avoid problems; instead we must recognize the need to work through them in ways that can help us accelerate in our God consciousness. When we find ourselves absorbed in a worry, we should take the time to reflect on the actual variables involved in the issue because this might help us develop a clearer insight and find a more positive way to respond to the situation. At the very least, we should clearly understand the reasons for our anxiety.

Sometimes spiritualists may struggle in their spiritual lives without even understanding the cause or the problem. If you ask them, "What is the problem?" they may simply respond, "I am not happy. I feel anxious and agitated." Then you might ask, "Well, what do you want to do? What is the issue?" Often they might reply, "I don't know. I just know that I do not want this service, but I don't know what I do want." Such a person may not have properly examined their own consciousness to discover the root cause of their dissatisfaction. We must look at our long and short-term goals to gain more clarity in our lives. Such introspection will help us take more responsibility for our own circumstances and appreciate God's arrangements and tests in our lives. After carefully weighing all of the facts, we can make more rational decisions. Although we might still make a poor decision in spite of having a plan, the clarity of vision will help us to fix the mistake or improve on the poor decision. However, if a cloud of anxiety covers our vision, we will continuously add to the cloud until it smothers or suffocates us.

Once we have made a careful decision, we should act and then beg for mercy and guidance. We have to act without being excessively attached to the outcome. There is always the element of risk in spiritual life. For this reason, Krishna told Arjuna:

iti te jnanam akhyatam
guhyad guhyataram maya
vimrsyaitad asesena
yathecchasi tatha kuru

Thus I have explained to you knowledge
still more confidential. Deliberate on
this fully, and then do what you wish
to do.

Bhagavad-gita 18.63

After hearing all the necessary instructions, Arjuna then
had the duty to act responsibly. This is the nature of free will.
However, our actions should not be foolishly based on mere
sentiment or unhealthy passion, but we should act according
to the *siddhanta*, the ultimate goal. We should do the necessary
according to *sadhu* (saints), *sastra* (scriptures), and *guru* (the
spiritual master). After considering the situation according to
these authorities, we must make decisions. Sometimes anxiety
results from a lack of decisiveness. Through a proper evalua-
tion, we will be able to make decisions or at least take responsibility for our actions.

When we feel tempted to worry about a problem, we should
first carefully answer the following questions:

• What is the actual problem?

• What is the cause of the problem?

• What are the possible solutions?

• What is the best solution that we can try to attain?

These questions can help us analyze the source of the anxiety that has absorbed our consciousness. Instead of allowing anxiety to overtake us, we can pinpoint the problem and try to understand the cause. After we have labeled the problem and considered possible solutions, the Lord in the heart often guides us if we accept His guidance. If we willingly put forth the necessary effort, we can also access the proper guidance from the Lord or from others.

Keep the Mind Busy

Keeping the mind busy is a valuable technique. Plenty of action is one of the best therapies or cures for a worrying mind. Many times we get absorbed in our anxieties because we do not have anything productive in which to engage our minds and bodies. All that loose energy needs to go somewhere. Therefore, a simple technique is to look at our use of time. When we are engaged in a healthy way, we will not be subject to such excessive amounts of anxiety.

Avoid the Trifles

We should carefully avoid worrying about the trifles that can ruin our happiness and faith in God, the spiritual master, and saints. Sometimes we have to be practical by trying to understand the probability of our worst fears actually happening. What are the chances that I will actually fall down and break my leg? It definitely happens but what are the chances?

Help and Serve Other People

An even greater way to avoid anxiety involves utilizing that energy to think of ways to help another person. We can put so much of our energy into finding ways to serve or assist someone else. There will always be another person whose problems far exceed our own. If we can relinquish some of our selfishness by trying to help another person in distress, we will not waste unnecessary energy in creating the exact problem that we want to avoid. By thinking about another person, we will naturally take our focus away from our own appetite and concerns, and this will actually cause us to become more powerful.

If we think too much about ourselves, we actually become powerless because we block God from coming through. As our selfishness increases, we will correspondingly lose our power in spiritual life because we will check God's real *sakti* or spiritual power from coming through in our lives. We will prevent the miracles that can occur when we remove our mental and physical disturbances and embrace divinity.

Understand the Influence of Karma

As we try to break this habit, sometimes we must recognize that a problem is beyond our control and we will have to deal with it as it is. A certain issue in our lives may just be a part of our *karma*. Some people do not have the *karma* to make much money in this lifetime. Other people can make simple investments that will automatically turn into large quantities of money due to their *karma*. One person can eat a regulated diet and exercise daily but cannot seem to make any improvement on their health. If it is a part of the person's *karma* to die at that time, he or she might even slip on a banana peel and die in spite of all the other endeavors to obtain good health. Considering the *karma* factor, we can try to change a situation if possible; otherwise, we may just have to accept our circumstances and let go of the worry.

Establish a Worry Time

Finally, we need to place boundaries to avoid an excessive

amount of anxiety. We may want to have a worry hour or time so that the worry, which may be such an integral part of us, can receive attention at a specific time. We can set aside one hour to worry about a problem and then move into another space after the allotted time period. Then the problem does not need to occupy our entire day but can be dealt with at a specific time. Furthermore, we want to constantly learn from the past while looking towards the future. Sometimes a worry deals solely with a problem or unfortunate situation from the past, but we do not want to remain in the past.

Looking into the Scriptures

Blazing Fire of Anxiety

The following scriptural references can provide us with deeper insights into this topic. *The Journey of Self-Discovery* describes the fire of anxiety within the heart:

> Everyone has a blazing fire within his heart—a blazing fire of anxiety. That is the nature of material existence. Always, everyone has anxiety; no one is free from it. Even a small bird has anxiety. If you give the small bird some grains to eat, he'll eat them, but he won't eat very peacefully. He'll look this way and that way—'Is somebody coming to kill me?' This is material existence. Everyone, even a president like Mr. Nixon, is full of anxieties, what to speak of others. Even Gandhi,

in our country—he was full of anxiety.
All politicians are full of anxiety. They
may hold a very exalted post, but still
the material disease—anxiety—is
there.
So if you want to be anxiety-less, then
you must take shelter of the *guru*,
the spiritual master. And the test of
the *guru* is that by following his
instructions you'll be free from anxiety.
This is the test. Don't try to find a cheap
guru or a fashionable *guru*. Just as you
sometimes keep a *guru* as a fashion—'I
have a *guru*'—that will not help. You
must accept a *guru* who can extinguish
the blazing fire of anxiety within your
heart. That is the first test of the *guru*.[1]

Some people want a *guru* who will pacify their consciousness and sanction their own ideas. Although they may succeed
in temporarily repressing their anxiety, it will still emerge at
a later time. However, if a person follows the instructions of
a bona fide *guru*, their anxiety will gradually decrease. The
actual problems may not necessarily decrease, and in some
cases, the problems may even increase, but at least we will
have a plan and faith in God as we do the necessary.

Anxiety for the Welfare of Other

In the *Srimad-Bhagavatam* 7.9.43, the great Vaisnava,
Prahlada Maharaja, prays to the Lord and displays his concern
for all humanity:

> O best of the great personalities, I am
> not at all afraid of material existence, for
> wherever I stay I am fully absorbed in
> thoughts of Your glories and activities.
> My concern is only for the fools and
> rascals who are making elaborate plans
> for material happiness and maintaining
> their families, societies and countries.
> I am simply concerned with love for
> them.

He had so much concern for the conditioned souls. A devotee's only anxiety should relate to the welfare of others. If we do not feel sympathy for the suffering of other living entities or feel anxious to spread Krishna consciousness, we should understand that our worries are excessive and unhealthy.

We may need to worry about our health, money, children or spouse, but we should always anxiously try to find ways to increase our quality of service. Otherwise, our unhealthy anxieties will actually produce more of what we do not want. Although devotees or servants of God should not deny a problem, their worries should never revolve around themselves. A devotee always anxiously tries to find ways to facilitate the spreading of God consciousness. Prahlada Maharaja exhibits the perfect use of anxiety by worrying about the highest welfare of other people.

Try to reflect on your anxieties and problems in your own way. Are your worries undefined? Are you developing plans to execute the proper action? Are your anxieties focused mainly on the bodily platform? Are you undermining God as the ultimate protector? In this way, we minimize God's grace that has already descended upon us. We will fail to see how the Lord has arranged everything in our environments for a specific purpose.

The Spiritual World is Without Anxiety

The purport of *Caitanya-caritamrta, Adi-lila* 7.74 states, "The spiritual world is called Vaikuntha, which means 'without anxiety.' In the material world everything is full of anxiety (*kuntha*), whereas in the spiritual world (Vaikuntha) everything is free from anxiety."[2]

The *Topmost Yoga System* discusses actual peacefulness. "Caitanya Mahaprabhu says that those who are Krishna conscious, because they have no demands, are actually peaceful. Those who are after sense enjoyment, salvation and yogic mystic perfection are always full of anxiety. As long as one is full of anxiety, one should know that he is still under the grip of material nature. And as soon as one is free from anxiety, one should know that he is liberated. This fearful anxiety exists because we do not know Krishna, the Supreme Lord and the supreme controller. Instead, we have other conceptions, and therefore we are always anxious."[3]

> All living entities—men, beasts, birds, or whatever—are always full of anxiety, and this is the material disease. If we are always full of anxiety, how can we attain peace? People may live in a very nice house, but out front they place signs saying, 'Beware of Dog,' or 'No Trespassers.' This means that although they are living comfortably, they are anxious that someone will come and molest them. Sitting in an

office and earning a very good salary,
a man is always thinking, 'Oh, I hope I
don't lose this position.' The American
nation is very rich, but because of this,
it has to maintain a great defense force.
So who is free from anxiety? The
conclusion is that if we want peace
without anxiety, we have to come to
Krishna consciousness. There is no
alternative.[4]

Anxiety is a major symptom of the material disease. If we
deny God's existence or deny His position as the supreme controller, we then push Him out of the way along with His love
and empowerment. We will even block the flow of blessings
coming from the previous *acaryas*.

A few of the devotee's qualifications
are further being described. No one is
put into difficulty, anxiety, fearfulness
or dissatisfaction by such a devotee.
Since a devotee is kind to everyone,
he does not act in such a way as to
put others into anxiety. At the same
time, if others try to put a devotee
into anxiety, he is not disturbed. It is
by the grace of the Lord that he is so
practiced that he is not disturbed by
any outward disturbance. Actually
because a devotee is always engrossed
in Krishna consciousness and engaged
in devotional service, such material

circumstances cannot move him.
Bhagavad-gita 12.15, purport

Keep in mind that a devotee should not feel anxious over his or her own problems but should feel extremely anxious for the well-being of others. Furthermore, a devotee should not act in a way that causes anxieties for other people. If we notice that our actions put another person into anxiety, which consequently hurts their spiritual life, we should examine our own behavior and try to make adjustments in a way that will minimize the negative effects on the person. This type of conscientiousness will signal our care and will support healthy association.

Reflect on your own life and consider the amount of anxiety saturating your existence. Can you define the level of anxiety in your life? Can you define the plans that you have for dealing with your worries? Are you engaged in some short-term goals, which can help lead you to the ultimate long-term goal of surrendering fully to God? If we do not plan, *maya* will plan for us. However, if we plan without faith in the Lord, *maya* will trick us and capture us again and again.

> Liberation, or *mukti*, means getting relief from these constant anxieties. This is possible only when the anxiety is changed to the devotional service of the Lord. *Srimad-Bhagavatam* gives us the chance to change the quality of anxiety from matter to spirit.
> *Srimad-Bhagavatam 1.12.28, purport*

Santaya: He has no anxiety. One who has to seek pleasure from other sources is always full of anxiety. *Karmis, jnanis* and *yogis* are full of anxiety because they want something, but a devotee does not want anything; he is simply satisfied in the service of the Lord, who is fully blissful.

Srimad-Bhagavatam 6.16.18-19, purport

So-called religious activities executed in the bodily conception of life are always accompanied by fear and anxiety about the ultimate result. But pure devotional service to the Supreme Personality of Godhead frees one from fear and anxiety because it is executed on the platform of Vaikuntha, or the spiritual place, where there is no fear or anxiety. According to Srila Jiva Gosvami, the process of *bhakti-yoga* is so powerful that even in the stage of *sadhana-bhakti,* in which one is practicing devotional service through rules and regulations, the neophyte can have a direct experience of fearlessness by the mercy of the Lord. As one's devotional service becomes mature, the Lord reveals Himself to the devotee, and all fear is totally vanquished forever.

Srimad-Bhagavatam 11.2.33 purport

Unless the living entity comes to the

guaranteed protection of the Su
Lord, he is full of anxiety. Th
of material anxiety is called m
existence. To be completely satisfied
and devoid of anxiety, one must come
to the position of eternally rendering
service to the Supreme Lord.

Caitanya-caritamrta,
Madhya-lila 1.206, purport

The difference between a person in
Krishna consciousness and a person
in bodily consciousness is that the
former is attached to Krishna whereas
the latter is attached to the results of his
activities. The person who is attached
to Krishna and works for Him only is
certainly a liberated person, and he
has no anxiety over the results of his
work. In the *Bhagavatam*, the cause of
anxiety over the result of an activity is
explained as being one's functioning
in the conception of duality, that is,
without knowledge of the Absolute
Truth.

Bhagavad-gita 5.12, purport

Once one surrenders unto the service
of the Supreme Lord, the Lord takes
charge of the maintenance of the
devotee's body, and there is no need
of anxiety for its protection. It is

said in the Second Chapter, Second
Canto, of *Srimad-Bhagavatam* that a
fully surrendered soul has no anxiety
about the maintenance of his body.
The Supreme Lord takes care of the
maintenance of innumerable species
of bodies; therefore, one who fully
engages in His service will not go
unprotected by the Supreme Lord.

Srimad-Bhagavatam 3.33.29, purport

Exemplary Personalities

Not only does the *Srimad-Bhagavatam* explain that one
must take full shelter of the Lord, but the many great personalities such as Pariksit Maharaja, a pure devotee King in ancient
times who was cursed to die by a snakebite, also lived this
instruction in a very real way. He had all types of reasons to feel
fearful since a snakebite would soon end his life, but he did not
feel anxious. Instead, he carefully engaged in the proper action.
As his death approached, he wanted to understand how to act.
Therefore, with rapt attention, he elevated his consciousness
by carefully hearing the instructions from Sukadeva Gosvami,
a young but highly advanced spiritual mentor.

Draupadi, another great personality from the *Mahabharata*
epic, also had ample reason to worry. In spite of the presence
of her husbands who were all powerful *ksatriyas* or warriors,
Duhsasana continued to try to disrobe her in the assembly hall,
an unbearable disgrace for a chaste woman. However, she took
the proper action by turning to God who supplied her with an
unlimited amount of cloth. On another occasion, when Durvasa

Muni, a mystic *yogi*, came to their forest residence with his numerous disciples and desired to eat, Draupadi once again had every reason to feel completely anxious. She did not know how she would feed all of those personalities and feared the sage's curse. However, she once again went into proper action, and by satisfying Krishna, all of her anxieties were eradicated. The great Vaisnava *acarya*, His Divine Grace A.C. Bhaktivedanta Swami Prabhupada, also exemplifies this exalted position. He came to America in 1965 at an old age with a sick body and did not know anyone or have any money; however, he went into proper action. He depended on God, who gave him amazing facilities and the ability to accomplish so much.

Sudama Vipra, a humble saint in the *Srimad-Bhagavatam*, did not have any material opulences due to his impoverished state but he did not fall into anxiety. Although his wife encouraged him to visit Krishna and ask for His help, Sudama agreed simply because he wanted the Lord's association. Therefore, when Sudama arrived at the Lord's palace in Dvaraka, he did not ask for any material boons but simply relished the Lord's association. However, when he returned to his home, he found an exorbitant amount of opulence and then praised the friendship of the Supreme Personality of Godhead. *Sri Caitanya-caritamrta* describes Kholaveca Sridhara, a poor vender, who also did not have any material commodities. He lived very meagerly by selling plantain leaves and only felt anxious to carry out his duty. He felt extremely happy to be able to serve Lord Caitanya who is considered in Gaudiya Vaisnavism to be the incarnation of the Supreme Lord. The Lord then embraced and blessed him.

Service to God

As we read through these many different pastimes, we will see how all of these great devotees acted in a way that would best please the Lord. They did not unnecessarily worry, doubt God's presence, or avoid the problem. Rather, a devotee considers how to act in a way that will bring out the best result and satisfy *guru* and Krishna. The devotee wants to find the best way to gain freedom from the material energy or *kuntha* and embrace the atmosphere of Vaikuntha. Excessive worry indicates that we are pushing God out of our lives and participating too much in the duality. When we absorb ourselves in anxiety, it indicates our lack of faith in God's personal concern and attentiveness to each of us individually. However, He is watching and is fully concerned. Our excessive anxieties also indicate our own cowardice because we have substituted worry for proper action.

Recently, my own body required a surgical operation. In the time leading up to my surgery, I received many letters and phone calls from devotees all over the world, anxious about the outcome. However, what is the anxiety about? The body is a body. What if the worst happens? Plan for that situation. Why are they not preparing themselves more to serve and help spread God consciousness more effectively? Why are they not trying to free themselves of any type of stagnation that connects us with the duality? We want to feel anxious to let God's mercy come into our lives. We should feel anxious to increase our level of service and use everything we have more resourcefully. We should feel anxious to plan instead of feeling lazy, sorrowful, depressed, or victimized. When these negative qualities increase in our lives, it means that we are basically telling Krishna, "You made a mistake." We want to say to God, "Your arrangements are perfect and whatever You arrange is due to Your mercy. I want to grab that mercy." We want to access that sort of greed. Too much anxiety means that we lack a sufficient amount of greed for the higher since we have involved ourselves excessively in the lower.

As we plan our short-term goals and move toward the long-term goals, we can use these techniques and scriptural references to help us avoid the pitfalls of anxiety. As we try to become doubtless, fearless, grave, and faithful, we will experience amazing reciprocation. We do not want to fall into a powerless situation by allowing this negative mind culture to attack and haunt us. It will try to convince us of God's absence in our lives. However, we want to allow the Supreme to work in our lives by developing proper gratitude and reflecting more on other people than ourselves.

Questions and Answers

Question: Thank you for giving us these helpful techniques. If we use our worry time to think of ways to help people, does this constitute worry?

Answer: That would be a good use of time. We must use strategy. Caitanya Mahaprabhu's whole mission is a mission of strategy and the Supreme Personality of Godhead constantly uses strategy when He descends in His many different incarnations. He has a reason for each particular incarnation and form. It is all part of His strategy to help the conditioned souls and to annihilate the demons. As a representative of the Lord, a devotee must act according to His mood by strategically preaching but he or she should still continue to address the essential aspects of life. We should think, "If I have sufficient money, I will be able to make so many different arrangements in Krishna's service. If I make this change, it will help my family focus more on God consciousness." Our meditation should always revolve around our service to God. If our worries selfishly revolve around our own body or circumstances, we will naturally lose enthusiasm to engage in the positive activities of devotional service. It will also cause us to block Krishna's blessings because He reciprocates with us when we make good use of what we have.

When we worry, we are basically telling God, "You gave to other people but You did not give to me. You showed kindness to that person but You denied me. Although You control so many situations, You left my situation up to Yamaraja, the superintendent of death." Such anxieties basically deny God's presence in our lives. For example, you might have a friend who constantly offers you help or assistance. He or she might bring you food or books, clean your house, and try to assist you in every way possible, but you simply give your friend complaints in return. These complaints basically indicate that you do not value the person's endeavors or services and see him or her as a part of your problem. In the same way, the Lord is offering us so much assistance, but instead of appreciating His current and past arrangements in our lives, we simply complain to Him. How can we have more abundance and success in our lives if we constantly meditate on our anxieties? If we just worry about what we do not have or what we want to happen, we will just feel miserable. How can we feel excited or enthused if we constantly tell ourselves that the Supreme has made mistakes in our lives? If we constantly tell ourselves that our lives have no value and we see ourselves as failures, how do we expect to develop value?

Question: You labeled one category of worriers as cowards who do not take action. I think that I fall into this category at different times. Sometimes I feel as if I should just be God conscious and not meditate on the body so much because we should remember our ultimate goal and act as an example of this goal. Although I know that we have the absolute, at times I am still a coward.

Answer: It is not wrong to worry about the body if it relates to God. If we worry about the body in terms of our service and connection to the Lord, we will also get inspiration about what to do in spite of the physical challenges. However, if we worry about the body as an individual entity, disregarding its connection with the Lord, such reflections will not transcend the bodily platform. When we worry about the body, we should reflect on its connection with our service in a genuine devotional attitude. If such reflections are genuine, we will receive some inspiration on how to help the problem or how to act in spite of the physical limitations. If our car breaks down, we want to fix the problem so that we can use it to buy groceries or in another service. This is a healthy worry. If you do not have any concern, you will not fix the problem. However, when we do address the problem, our energy should revolve around proper planning according to the spiritual nucleus. As personalists, we do scrutinize and reflect because we want to receive blessings in our service and raise our consciousness. These factors are all very important.

Lord Caitanya felt anxiety to help the conditioned souls and we also have to utilize some of that anxiety in order to make ourselves better servants. We just need to examine the underlying motivation for our worry. Do we feel anxiety because of our inability to enjoy and satisfy our senses or do we feel anxious to become better servants of God? We may have genuine limitations and worries but we will never be in a situation in which we cannot serve, even if we can only offer service mentally.

Question: You mentioned that a devotee should not put another person into anxiety. When another devotee puts me into anxiety, it seems that my own false ego may cause more anxiety than the actual actions of the other person. How do I understand my level of responsibility in codifying the actions of another devotee?

Answer: We just discussed in the *Bhagavad-gita* that a devotee does not experience anxiety or put others into anxiety. Of course, it is not possible for anyone to never cause anxiety to another because, in spite of our best intentions, our actions may agitate another person. However, we should intend to do or say the proper thing in the most tactful way. Although a devotee considers the perceptions of other people, he or she does not avoid speaking or acting properly according to *sastra* or scripture. We do not want to take this point to an unhealthy extreme by thinking, "I will simply avoid speaking the truth because if I speak *sastra* and live it, I may agitate someone." What can we do? Although we should try to find a tactful way to speak or act in order to minimize the agitation, we cannot change our principles. For instance, if someone is disturbed by our principle of vegetarianism, we do not decide to eat meat as a way to avoid agitating them. However, we do want to act in a way that will minimize their misunderstanding or offenses.

In this way, we can try to discover the source of our anxiety. Do we feel disturbed due to the element of false ego or do we feel anxiety because someone has misunderstood our endeavor to act as proper servants? Even that type of anxiety is unhealthy because we should constantly find ways to improve on our service. That type of anxiety could even lead us into the pity game or cause us to act without a genuine concern for the well-being of another person. If we act for the benefit of another but they do not appreciate our endeavor to assist them, we should find better ways to execute our purpose. We should not feel depressed or remorseful if no one accepts our endeavors because such remorsefulness simply indicates that we want appreciation rather than genuine service.

Question: I have a question in relation to Prahlada Maharaja's prayers. I always thought that anxiety for people who do not follow a spiritual path indicates a lack of faith. For instance, if we worry too much about a family member who does not have a devotional consciousness, doesn't it indicate our lack of faith in God by trying to control the situation ourselves since He ultimately takes care of everyone?

Answer: We understand that everyone is on the Lord's path and a first class devotee does not even make a distinction. However, in order to preach, one anxiously wants to encourage people to recognize God's presence at a faster pace. The preacher wants to speed up the process by encouraging a person to work through whatever he or she needs to experience or learn. That anxiety is healthy if we sufficiently devise a plan to help such people; otherwise, the anxiety is unhealthy. Sometimes we can only help a person through a good example and through kindness but this also requires strategy.

Question: Sometimes we feel hesitation, fear or anxiety, which does not necessarily come from the immediate external level but from an unconscious level. Such anxieties may even disturb our sleep so that we do not feel properly rested. How do we uproot this type of anxiety?

Answer: Some anxieties often relate to the subconscious mind as it responds to stimuli in the environment. If we are more attentive in our *sadhana* or spiritual practices and in our daily activities, it will affect the activities in the subconscious. We should try to listen to tapes with more attention, intensely pray with more absorption, and engage in our services with more appreciation. Such mindful activities will penetrate deeper and deeper into the subconscious mind. At times, when we feel extremely anxious and cannot seem to harness the mind, we can pray to the Lord to help us see the situation differently. Sometimes if a situation continues to bother us, we just have to pray to Krishna or God for help in removing any blocks in our service.

Question: I want to also offer one technique that has assisted me in the last twenty years. When I catch myself worrying too much, I just pray and ask the Lord to do the worrying for me.

Answer: In one sense, it actually makes the Lord your servant. For now it helps you but you do not want to hold onto it because a devotee will even worry if it pleases God. However, I see that you want to try to turn the worry over to the Lord but it is better to ask Him to help you plan properly for the proper action and then even thank Him. Sometimes when we have an anxiety, we should just thank God for bringing the circumstance to us and thank Him for allowing us to undergo this situation instead of something much worse. By asking God to worry for us, we will minimize our gratitude.

Chapter 2

Choosing Love Over Fear

kamo manyur mado lobhah
soka-moha-bhayadayah
karma-bandhas ca yan-mulah
svikuryat ko nu tad budhah

The mind is the root cause of lust, anger, pride, greed, lamentation, illusion and fear. Combined, these constitute bondage to fruitive activity. What learned man would put faith in the mind?

Srimad-Bhagavatam 5.6.5

Increasing Societal Fears

The culture of fear, which is quite powerful and almost all-encompassing, is actually sweeping the planet at this time. Fear is such a powerful ingredient in the material energy. As a matter of fact, the Vedic paradigm considers fear to be one of the major factors that maintains the material world and the illusion. We have already described the four basic engagements that the living entities pursue instead of self-realization—eating, sleeping, mating, and fearing or defending. All species of life must eat and sleep in order to gain strength and rejuvenate the body. Mating is also a natural function necessary for the growth and development of a species. However, while the living entities pursue these activities, they constantly fear that such activities will cease or the quality of eating, sleeping, and mating will decrease. Consequently, they always have an underlying fear of the future.

The Vedic scriptures also describe the specific types of miseries or fears that attack all living entities regardless of their race, tribe, gender, or place of residence. The basic miseries are known as *adhyatmika*, *adhidaivika*, and *adhibhautika*. *Adhyatmika* refers to the attacks or fears created by one's own mind. The fears which result from the *devas* or demigods and the environment such as hurricanes, tornadoes, earthquakes, droughts, or floods are known as *adhidaivika*. Some of these torments can attack us abruptly and even have such devastating power that they take our lives. Due to negative circumstances that we may have undergone in the past, we maintain a sense of fear in the present and carry that into the future. The last type of fear, *adhibhautika*, results from our interactions with other people and from the constant disappointments or disturbances that we experience through the process of socialization.

Unless people take tremendous shelt
culture and repeatedly surcharge themselv
fears will remain an integral part of their l
as Kali-yuga or the Age of Quarrel and Hy
the influence of fear will also concomitantly increase. Not only
are we products of this fear, but our children and grandchildren must also grow up in this environment, which we help to
maintain in our own ways. To the extent that we fail to embrace
love, we will simultaneously create and maintain the culture of
fear. Eating, sleeping, mating, and fearing along with the three
miseries are all a part of this illusory culture.

The terrorist attacks on September 11, 2001 have escalated
people's fears and anxieties, since the devastation has exposed
some of these illusions. Those illusions that seemed enduring
and dependable can no longer offer the same sense of security.
Although some people feel that these attacks have changed the
world, in another sense our predicament has always been the
same because these three miseries, *adhyatmika*, *adhidaivika*,
and *adhibhautika*, have always harassed the world. People
have always focused their attention on eating, sleeping, mating, and fearing, but sometimes in different parts of the world
the cosmetic façade covers the reality of the situation.

As we move into the twenty-first century, we will definitely
see an increase in environmental fears. We hear about tampered
medicine, mad cow disease, killer bees, serial killers, asbestos,
terrorists, and nuclear and chemical warfare. Cancer, AIDS, and
heart disease are taking many lives, and certain places are suffering from droughts, cyclones, and hurricanes. There is even
an increase in mental disturbances such as varieties of depres-
sions, anxieties, and mental illnesses. The amount of violence
and hostility is rapidly escalating. The terrorists are also causing extensive fear, especially due to the attacks on the World

Trade Center, which claimed a massive number of lives.

The book, *Fear Less*, by Gavin de Becker, offers us a clearer idea of the amount of violence that prevails throughout the United States:

> In the past two years alone, more Americans died from gunshot wounds than were killed during the entire Vietnam War—ten times the number who died at the World Trade Center...For example, in all of Japan, the number of young men shot to death in a year is equal to the number killed in New York City in a single busy weekend...When four jumbo jets crashed on September 11 we were deeply shaken, but imagine that a jumbo jet full of passengers crashed every single month, month in and month out. The number of people killed still wouldn't equal the number of American women murdered by their husbands and boyfriends each year.[5]

Since people must live amidst such hostility and violence, they constantly feel fearful due to the realities of the situation. Consequently, we need to have a complete internal revolution on this planet. All over the world people are waging all types of wars between individuals and between countries. We need spiritual soldiers who can counteract these negative forces. For this reason, I am writing this series of books entitled *Spiritual Warrior*. People need to understand how this negative culture affects their families and environments, and will gradually infiltrate the present human consciousness on this planet until it literally creates a different species. Even now the negative propaganda that we constantly see and hear is altering our current state of existence because it is changing our priorities and even stimulating our hidden priorities. We need to strategize in order to wage peace instead of war. We should not simply withdraw but we must form a strategy to protect ourselves and raise our consciousness in order to alleviate some of this extensive fear. This is the clarion call for spiritual warfare.

The Miseries of Material Nature

When I visited Mauritius in 2002, a small country in the Indian Ocean, a cyclone suddenly manifested out of the ocean. The Vedic scriptures say that these cyclones, hurricanes, or tornados are living entities and I could understand this for the first time through the experience. A cyclone is extremely powerful and almost sounds like the screams, yells, and whistles of a person. Houses, trees, and cars were just tossed around and people were even dying. It is comparable to the mood of an angry person who suddenly increases their attacks and then decides to finish off the assault. The cyclone even left at one point but then returned to do more damage.

The people were very fearful because the previous cyclones had devastating effects and they realized that the current cyclone would also cause extensive damage. They were apprehensively wondering whose house, building, or body would suffer from this attack. For almost four days, the electricity and water was shut off and most of the roads were blocked by debris or flooded.

After I left Mauritius, I read a newspaper on the plane

that described an accident in Nigeria. At one military base, a series of bombs exploded which devastated citizens of their own country. The bombs just blew away homes and people, and for many hours, people thought that the world might end. Thousands of people died in this single accident.

During one of my visits to Bosnia and Croatia, I talked to some of my disciples there about the atmosphere during the war. They explained how they had seen twenty or thirty people die right in front of them after a bomb dropped in a downtown area. One of the bombs even destroyed half of a devotee's home while she was in the house. They then described the number of women who were raped or abused and the number of fathers, sons, and brothers who were killed.

Can you imagine the type of trauma that one experiences during such an intense war? Can you imagine the type of fear that people feel in that environment? Can you imagine what these people pass on to those connected with them such as their children or grandchildren? We now understand how alcoholic parents affect their children in a very direct way. Parents who have AIDS or took crack during pregnancy also affect their children due to the physiological, psychological, and karmic connection. Consequently, this consciousness of fear affects every aspect of people's lives. They transmit this consciousness to their children, which then permeates throughout the global community. Whether the attacks come from one's own issues, from the effects of the *devas* or from social interactions, these are very dangerous times.

We want to closely examine this issue in order to help you, the reader, as well as myself so that our consciousness can make a difference. During war, the causes of fear are often specifically organized to harness people's consciousness and coerce them to act. In the course of this discussion, you will see how love cannot develop sufficiently in the presence of fear. It will prevent you from becoming your best because you will not be able to give the best that you have. Although you can try to love despite the fear, it will inevitably create various types of blockages.

The Three Types of Fear

As we reflect on our lives, we will see that at practically every hour of the day, our minds engage in some type of fearing. We constantly worry about the future according to our past experiences along with our present circumstances. In a recent workshop, I asked the students to list their greatest fears from each of the three categories—*adhyatmika*, *adhidaivika*, and *adhibhautika*. Each person has their own stock of fears, which they carry with them everywhere. In relation to the fears stemming from the mind, one student had a reoccurring fear that the Lord would force him into displeasing situations or force him to act against his own desire. He also feared that some unwanted calamity might happen in his life. He recognizes it as a fear in the mind and understands that sometimes he might just have to go through a distressing situation. In this case, it is a fear of God's power and a fear that God will execute His own plan rather than the plan of the individual. He fears that God's plan may cause displeasure.

Another student revealed that she has a tremendous fear of making mistakes and embarrassing herself. She also fears that other people may not support or appreciate her actions. Several people felt fear of abandonment by those who they love. Fear of abandonment affects many people because although the people who we love the most can make us the happiest, we know that our closest associates can also hurt us the most. Try to remember the times in which you felt the most depressed, disappointed, or anxious. What caused such intense emotions? Usually, such feelings stem from the person we love the most. Our employee or associate can hurt us but not to the same degree as the person we care for most deeply. When we try to care for another person and have expectations of reciprocation, we will feel much more hurt when that reciprocation does not manifest.

Fears stemming from the mind can also include an intense fear of failure because of how others will think of them and what it will mean in terms of their identity in the environment. They fear how people will categorize them according to their low achievement. Another person may fear success because it might put them into a certain position that others may not appreciate and support. As a result, they may even lose their friendships with some people. The mind is so powerful that whatever thoughts we have on a regular basis will obviously determine how we speak and act. The mind can be so powerful with its creative function, but the same mind can be excessively vicious and destructive.

After analyzing the fears in the mind, I then requested the group to share their fears stemming from the environment. Although every fear has some type of connection with the mind, some fears have more specific causes. Some common responses included fears of death, heights, darkness, and thunder. Then we examined fears of other living entities. Such responses included a fear of thieves and doctors. One student felt fearful of his mother-in-law. Others felt fearful of bad association and of negligent drivers on the road who might cause accidents. Someone felt fearful for the children. One person expressed a deep fear of giving their heart and having it broken. Although many people have this type of fear, many do not because they do not give their hearts; therefore, they miss the risk and adventure of deep affectionate relationships.

Hope and Fear

Interestingly, we can make a distinct correlation between fear and hope. During these same workshops, some of the students shared their one greatest fear, which might belong to any one of these three categories. Several responses included a fear of uncertainty in life, a fear of the death of one's children or mother, a fear of a spiritual fall down, fear of abandonment by the spiritual master, and a fear of one's own death. I then requested the same individuals to share their deepest hopes, which often directly oppose our greatest fears. For instance, the person who feared for the death of their child also strongly hopes for the well-being of the child. If you could have a magic wand, what would you most want to see happen in your life? Your greatest hope would probably relate to your greatest fear.

By analyzing each of these fears, their connection to hope will manifest more clearly. Someone felt most fearful of uncertainty. If he reflects on his greatest hope, he would probably want certainty in his life. The person who fears a spiritual fall down probably intensely hopes to never stray from the spiritual path. The devotee who fears abandonment by her spiritual master would most desire to have her spiritual mentor always present. Fear of death is, however, rather natural since no one lives forever, but it should not be excessive. From these examples, we can see that our greatest desire will often oppose our greatest fear.

Our fears often revolve around those things that we most

value. For instance, we may fear that a situation will not unfold according to our desires and we often place so much of our mental energy into such an anxiety. This type of mentality is dangerous because if it begins to encompass us and form a part of our internal dialogue, we may even cause our worst fears to manifest. The mind is even more powerful than our physical actions and our speech. The subconscious mind does not always recognize the difference between a positive and a negative; it simply hears the continuous flow of thoughts. For instance, if we try to overcome an addiction but just continue to repeatedly tell ourselves to stop the bad habit, our constant meditation on it may even lead to more of the same negative patterns. The subconscious mind normally only receives an impression of what you present to it instead of distinguishing between the negative and the positive.

Further Divisions of Fear

We can also divide fear into five other distinct categories. We do not simply want to make a psychological presentation but this information may prove to be a valuable asset for those of you on a spiritual path because it can enable you to help others. Although it is helpful to understand how fear can affect you, such knowledge will also help you understand the symptoms that people have when they suffer from these attacks. We want to act as spiritual warriors in order to counteract some of the negativity that is sweeping the world.

1. **General anxieties** have a strong effect on the mind and body, and can even interfere with a person's spiritual life. General anxieties often lead to insomnia or even night-

mares. It can affect the heart or lead to fainting spells, dizziness, and trembling. Such anxieties can also make people very fearful in their relationships.

2. **Panic** is a part of the manifestation of the culture of fear on this planet. Some people even suffer from a specific disorder known as panic attacks. The symptoms include headaches, shortness of breath, nausea, sweating, quivering, shaking, heart palpitations, and vomiting. A person may feel as though they might die. These are very serious symptoms that affect the mind and body and can even extend for a long period of time. Millions of people suffer from these types of attacks or will suffer from them in the next few years.

3. Millions of people suffer from **obsessive-compulsive disorders**, which also manifest from fear. These obsessive-compulsive activities occur in some people who feel forced to constantly do the same activities over and over. They simply cannot avoid the behavior. For example, a person might be afraid of contracting a disease; therefore, they spend hours just washing their hands. Another person may be afraid to leave a door unlocked, and as a result, he or she must check the front door repeatedly before leaving the house. Even though they might recognize such behavior to be irrational, they simply cannot control themselves. Since they have imbibed the culture of fear, they simply act accordingly.

4. **Phobias** can have a devastating effect on a person's life. A person who suffers from a phobia must live every day under the influence of heavy fears. For instance, some

people are afraid of heights and other people are afraid of small or confined spaces. A claustrophobic may not be able to sit in a crowded room for even a short period of time. If they do manage to stay in the room, they would probably have to sit near a door so that they could easily escape in an emergency. When they end up in a confined room that does not have an easy escape route, they may sweat, shake, faint, or vomit out of fear.

5. **Posttraumatic stress** results from a previous trauma or hurt. For instance, reports indicate that 20% of women and 5-10% of men experience some form of sexual abuse as children, which means that many young girls and boys must deal with these issues.[6] Since their so-called protectors exploited them, many of them lack trust in authority and cannot really give themselves in a relationship. Many of them feel intense fear and anger toward themselves and toward others. They even have to deal with dysfunctional issues in terms of sex life due to the posttraumatic effects that carry over. Some people suffer from this fear to such an extent that it acts as an anchor and forces them to relive that experience again and again.

Millions of people in America alone suffer from fear in these particular ways. Unfortunately, as these people interact, they drop their fears into the environment and onto their associates. For instance, parents who carry these anxieties with them end up dropping these negative emotions directly onto their children or spouse. A phobic person is rarely able to be fully present or sufficiently loving since they are emotionally shut down. People suffering from wounds cannot give their full love, especially if they are afraid to open their hearts or honestly address their past. We cannot raise our own consciousness sufficiently or the consciousness of others if the duality of fear and aggression has captured our minds. Fear allows *maya* or evil to enter deep into a person's consciousness because it destroys the shield of love that blocks or eliminates the attack. Once the shield of love disintegrates, the fear will increase and present its strongest attacks. We do not want to allow fear's attacks to wound or devastate us; therefore, we must constantly strengthen our internal constitution.

Posttraumatic Stress within Spiritual Communities

Due to very devastating experiences that spiritual seekers can encounter while serving in spiritual communities and institutions which can later lead to serious posttraumatic stress, we want to elaborate on this fear in more detail. Many people suffer from these traumatic experiences due to abuse and exploitation that they underwent within religious communities. In such cases, overcoming the problem will become more challenging because the person will have a harder time taking shelter of the religion or institution. The person might even undergo this intense experience when he or she enters the environment or participates in certain religious practices. Therefore, we want to offer ways in which such people can regain their faith.

It is most unfortunate when a person fears the exact medicine that will help him or her. First we will put forth two secular examples and then two spiritual examples of such situations to help us understand how posttraumatic stress develops. In our first scenario, Jim needs to swim constantly since he is the captain of the swimming team; however, due to a particular trauma that happened to him in the water several years ago, he has developed a fear of water and feels intense stress when he comes close to large bodies of water. Another example involves Dr. Goldman, a surgeon, who used to operate on a daily basis. However, due to an abuse perpetrated by his supervisor, whenever he entered into the operating room, he experienced posttraumatic stress and had to quit his job.

The two other scenarios involve abuse within religious communities. Mary attended a convent, and during a retreat, an elderly nun molested her. Consequently, she now experiences posttraumatic stress attacks whenever she sees any nuns over forty years of age. Our last example involves a *brahmana* who was studying in an *asrama* in Europe under the guidance of a seemingly very powerful *guru*. He later found out that this *guru* was deviating in many ways, which caused some internal turmoil since he had deep faith in the *guru* and had fully accepted him as his mentor. After hearing of these deviations, he fell into depression for quite some time. Although he has been able to somewhat cope with his depression, he has not be able to transcend his posttraumatic stress attacks which he encounters every time he enters into a temple and sees certain aspects of the spiritual culture that remind him of the *guru*.

After examining a few ways in which posttraumatic stress can develop, we will provide some considerations to help people through these difficult moments. We especially want to look at ways to help those having anxiety attacks and great fear due to similarly inauspicious experiences that happened to them in connection with spiritual communities or institutions. It is very difficult for anyone suffering from abuse or exploitation in any form; however, it is even worse when a person's life or profession has been altered due to such atrocities. Unfortunately, it is most devastating for those who have lost faith in the spiritual journey, are afraid to engage in spiritual practices, or fear spiritual association that could move them distinctly toward self-actualization. The following techniques can help a person deal with posttraumatic stress associated with such problems:

1. **Scrutinize the philosophy in order to determine whether or not it is inherently unhealthy.** If people find themselves in an abusive situation, they must learn the science of how to look for authentic religion and authentic community. They should separate themselves from harmful associations.

2. **Understand the difference between the philosophy and the deviations.** There are obviously times when the philosophy and theology is sound but certain aspects of the environment are unproductive and even degrading. In such cases, one must endeavor to separate some of the negative sociological influences from the philosophy and theology itself.

3. **Reflect on the many good experiences within the community.** Although a person may reside in a healthy community, he or she can still experience some abuse or exploitation from certain deviant individuals. However, to avoid excessive anxiety, one can reflect on the many wonderful experiences in the past.

4. **Practice forgiveness.** Forgiveness is always very important so that we can live more in the present and for the future without allowing the past to constantly haunt us.

5. **Allow cognitive reconditioning.** The person can assimi-

late experiences in a less threatening environment. In other words, if we are suffering from posttraumatic stress attacks while worshiping in a religious setting due to previous abuse associated with that place, for a period of time the worship should be done in different, non-threatening settings.

6. **Visualize yourself in the environment.** People can visualize themselves in the previous environment, but in this case, they see themselves doing well without any stress or negativity.

7. **Visit the environment with a loved one.** Those who are closest to us provide great solace. If we can make short visits to difficult places with a loved one, it can minimize or gradually eliminate the problem.

8. **Study the saints of the theology closer.** We can learn so much from closer study of the bona fide saints in terms of how they dealt with all types of challenges.

9. **Pray and ask God for help.** We should always ask the Lord to help us gain different perspectives in dealing with all types of problems.

10. **Know that God does not want you to live in fear.** Fear interferes with our ability to learn and receive the love that God is sending.

Consequences of Fear

Fear can sicken and weaken our bo
adrenaline in the entire body because it is a
malistic tendency to eat, sleep, mate, and defend. When an animal is fearful, adrenaline causes changes in its body because it
is preparing to fight or to flee. Psychologists call this response
the fight-or-flight syndrome. The adrenaline causes the blood
to clot in such a way that will enable the body to better contain
the blood if a person or animal suffers from a wound. Fear also
causes our neurotransmitters to send messages that can cause
the body's defenses to attack its own organs.

Furthermore, living in the past hurts us because it means
that we are allowing an unfortunate situation to attack us
again and again and are minimizing our ability to fully live in
the present. Fear can prevent us from deeply loving another
person. Although you may want to deeply love, that fear will
present many blocks. You will not give yourself fully and this
will also prevent the other person from giving him or herself
fully. How can people fully give themselves when this culture
of fear bombards them consciously or unconsciously every
single day? Considering these factors, it should not surprise us
to see more and more relationships falling apart. These factors
also contribute to the abuse of women, children, and the elderly
because people constantly hear about such violence from so
many sources. They read about it in the papers, listen to it on
the news, and watch such violence in the movie theaters. This
culture of fear is bombarding them in many ways, and this is
very dangerous. There is no shortage of demonic leaders who
know the effects of such bombardments and eagerly support
this negativity in order to keep us divided and disempowered.

The government is currently warning us against terrorism

and telling us to act cautiously in our daily lives. Although these attacks are a reality that is disturbing the nation, much of the fear is meant to create more of a negative world order based on fear. When people become very fearful and animalistic, they can act in vicious ways. Furthermore, fear prevents us from connecting with other people on deeper levels because we may resort to interpolation and speculation. In conjecturing about the needs of a person, it can consequently produce unsatisfactory or even harmful results.

Endeavor for Transformation Rather Than Reformation

In order to try to mitigate these fears, some people have taken to social activism, but in spite of their endeavors, they mainly just address the manifestations in the external world. They encourage a type of revolution that deals more with reformation than with a real sense of transformation. Although they want to change the people, change the political strata, and change certain environmental problems, this type of change does not really surpass the mundane platform since it does not focus on internal growth and nourishment. Other people may want to grow internally and will chant their prayers, engage in their meditation, and access their divine interventions through channeling to address their own concerns, but they fail to consider the sufferings of other people.

Neither the social activists nor the selfish spiritualists are really engaged in acts of pure love and peace. The problems are far beyond physical appearances and acts of spiritual selfishness. The problems have always related to the community and to the planet instead of only to the individual. People who try to engage solely in their own realization or in their own contact with God are not really mature spiritualists. The Supreme Lord Himself surely does not act in this way. He constantly sends representatives and arranges for the presence of *sadhu*, *sastra*, and *guru*. Even though many people do not accept Krishna's help, He still makes arrangements to try to assist as many people as possible.

A representative of God is one who acts according to God's will. The representatives must also genuinely care for other people, but their endeavor to care will remain sentimental unless they spiritually rejuvenate themselves. People need to develop their internal essence and nourish their souls through their own *sadhana* or spiritual practices. They need to engage in contemplative and introspective activities while endeavoring to enliven themselves spiritually. Then they will be able to influence the environment.

We should not think that social activism and personal salvation alone are sufficient to make a difference. People need to move beyond their own "isms," political involvements, cultural insights, and even their self-centered spiritual pursuits if they want to allow genuine spirituality to influence the environment. In order to accomplish this task, people must be able to recognize the elements of destruction and devastation, which include fear.

Love Versus Fear

Sigmund Freud also recognized that people have two basic emotions or instinctive activities. For instance, although people instinctively have the tendency to destroy, devastate, annihilate, and even kill, they also have the tendency to consolidate and maintain. He could also understand that the negative tendencies are based on fear and the positive activities are based on love or the search for love.

In my book, *Spiritual Warrior II*, I focus on transforming lust into love. In the scriptures, we recognize the existence of *prema* or ultimate pure love of God, which manifests in different ways. When that love comes in touch with the material energy and the duality, it temporarily turns into lust. This means that the insatiable desire to satisfy lust in this material world is actually misdirected love. Our potential to love has gone in the wrong direction. One metaphysical system known as *A Course in Miracles* explains that there is only love and fear.[7] Anything that interferes with love is negative and is only due to fear. Qualities such as lust, anger, envy, and greed are all connected with fear.

As I wrote in *Spiritual Warrior II*, every negative action is a cry for love and every positive action is a manifestation of love. If we simply categorize a negative action as negative, we will lock ourselves into that duality and even reinforce it. If your beloved feels envious and you categorize it negatively, you will not be able to have a healthy resolution. However, if we see the person's envy as a cry for attention and affection, we will have the ability to deal with him or her in a positive way. Your own words and actions may have caused your beloved to feel unloved which then turned into envy or jealousy. When someone expresses anger, we can simply label it as anger or we can see it as a cry for love or as an expression of fear. Try to see how these seemingly negative emotions are cries for love. Try to find ways to bring out this love.

For instance, we can simply label these terrorists as demons, but if we look closer at some of their biographies, we will also discover their own cries for love. In one case, the father of one of the terrorists would often call his son a sissy. His father wanted him to become a doctor but he could not reach this goal. He grew up feeling useless with no sense of value; therefore, he must have constantly felt hungry for a sense of identity and a sense of accomplishment. When some of these people hear that they can immediately attain paradise by dying in a religious war, they eagerly embrace this philosophy since their lives are already so full of suffering. Such a negative upbringing practically acts as a breeding ground for this type of fanatical mentality.

When we consider the crimes of such people, we must certainly mete out the necessary chastisements, but as spiritualists, we should go deeper and try to discover the real cause behind their actions. Even if we look at the most destructive serial killers, we will also discover that they have come from abusive backgrounds and then abused others as a way to gain a certain level of power. Their own feeling of powerlessness may now cause them to victimize weaker people. Their cry for love and affection has manifested in perverse ways and has covered over their desire for love. We can constantly look for the love factor that needs to be addressed in all of our interactions so that we can try to make a real difference.

The Evil Dog and the Good Dog

I would like to conclude this section with a Native American parable. Certain Native American tribes understand that there is an evil dog and a good dog within each person who continuously fight. The dog we feed the most will usually win. This same phenomenon goes on in our own lives because we all have a lower nature and a higher nature. We all have the choice to fear and to remain in a combative mindset by viewing others as adversaries. We have the choice to remain in a negative mindset by struggling to fulfill our desires because we fear that if we do not make our own arrangements, no one else will help us, not even God. Conversely, we have the choice to engage in proper action instead of just worrying or justifying our lack of action. We have the choice to look deeper into the problems on this planet instead of just trying to change them through social activism, which only alters the externals. We also do not want to fall into the category of selfish spiritualists who only concern ourselves with our own salvation. We want to engage in a total revolution, which is ultimately an internal revolution that then manifests in the environment in a healthy way.

When we realize that we can simply fall into the loving embrace of the Lord, we can avoid fear on all levels. By acting in the proper way, we will receive the best results because the Supreme Lord is not unfair. If we act properly in spite of the circumstances, we will receive reciprocation because, as we surrender to the Lord, He will reward and support us accordingly.

ye yatha mam prapadyante
tams tathaiva bhajamy aham
mama vartmanuvartante
manusyah partha sarvasah

As all surrender unto Me, I reward them
accordingly. Everyone follows My path
in all respects, O son of Prtha.
Bhagavad-gita 4.11

We readily avoid the sinful activity and embrace the proper

action, knowing that the indwelling presence of the Lord in the heart will accommodate the proper action. As we have more faith in the Supreme Personality of Godhead, our level of fear will naturally decrease.

The Culture of Fear

The world is at war. It is a very serious time due to the massive thrust toward this culture of fear that causes people to put their guards down and act according to their lower nature. This culture of fear causes them to feed the evil dog, which then puts anxiety into the environment and makes it easier to control people. Fear can lead to all kinds of irrational behavior because people will simply want to save themselves or want to force something to happen in their own way. They lose a sense of community, which involves serving and caring for each other, and they end up fixing their minds only on their own particular concerns or ideas. For many people, even their relationships do not work because they do not act as genuine partners. They are not ready to accept and trust the other person. When people develop spiritual relationships within institutions or with the spiritual master, they often lack authenticity because of a lack of love. It often revolves around manipulation, utilitarianism, and exploitation. The relationship will develop out of fear if people use others to try to build up their own sense of protection. This goes on in commerce, education, and also in spirituality. Most people are selfish due to fear that is smothering the world.

In your own lives, try to avoid falling into these patterns; otherwise, the amazing current of fear that is sweeping the planet and causing people to absorb themselves more in eating, sleeping, mating, and fearing will sweep you away. It is gradually becoming a more dominant aspect of Kali-yuga. For this reason, people take to a harsher lifestyle. Their loving propensity has been shut down and transformed into fear.

Questions and Answers

Question: How should we unlock the subconscious blocks that continue to affects us? Certain patterns continue to repeat in my life although I am not even conscious of why they happen. Although I am trying to focus spiritually and think positive, I realize that a certain blockage is inhibiting my progress.

Answer: If you see me continuously placing my hand in a fire and burning myself, you would probably wonder why I keep repeating the same action. Nevertheless, if I continue to follow the same patterns, I will continue to get the same results. These repeated activities often indicate that we have the same level of consciousness, and consequently, we will continue to receive a similar response.

How do we deal with these patterns? If our current environment reinforces these patterns, we may need to change our associations because sometimes our associates affect us in negative ways. In our endeavor to spiritually rejuvenate ourselves, we should try to bond with like-minded people so that they can reinforce our goals and we can learn from them. We can also compare these patterns to a drug addiction. For instance, an addict knows that certain associations, environments, and mindsets will rekindle their addiction. If after recovering they go through a period of sadness or loneliness, they may search for that artificial stimulation in order to fill the emptiness.

There are three psychological perceptions that can also

help an individual deal with any of his or her problems. These perceptions include **personal assertion, putting oneself in the other person's shoes**, and **disassociation**. Love is not just a matter of conceptualization. It involves our words, actions, and thoughts. When a problem arises in a relationship, you may need to apply personal assertion by personally involving yourself and trying to help. At other times, it is necessary to put yourself in the other person's shoes. You should not only think about the problem but also try to visualize yourself in the other person's position. Consider the way in which they would respond to your own words and actions. For example, if you have an argument with your spouse or child, you have choices. You can continue to see your own position as right, which may be necessary at times, but you can also take the time to consider how the other person may have perceived your own actions. Simply by considering the other person's views, you may gain an entirely different perspective on the situation.

We referred to the last perception as disassociation. There are times when you just need to disassociate yourself by watching your actions and the actions of the other person from a distance. This will help us look closer at ourselves and others with less prejudice and attachment, and will open our minds to additional possibilities. In this way, you can bring much more to the situation by acting in a loving way. In some cases, we can act lovingly by first trying to understand the other person's thoughts and actions. Such a reflection may shock us because it may reveal our own level of selfishness and fear. Often, we only think about what we want.

These three perceptions may help us in our endeavor to alter our consciousness and to always accept that the Supreme Personality of Godhead has made arrangements for our ultimate benefit. If the events in our lives do not benefit us in any way, then God is extremely cruel. It would mean that God lets people undergo all types of negative situations without any concern for them. Why serve such a God who allows such negative circumstances to happen in spite of our endeavors to serve Him? However, we understand that God is always in control.

aham sarvasya prabhavo
mattah sarvam pravartate
iti matva bhajante mam
budha bhava-samanvitah

I am the source of all spiritual and material worlds. Everything emanates from Me. The wise who perfectly know this engage in My devotional service and worship Me with all their hearts.
Bhagavad-gita 10.8

God controls the material as well as the spiritual, which means that everything directly or indirectly happens through the sanction of the Lord. If we can just accept that our circumstances are meant to benefit us, we will be able to connect with the loving aspect of the Lord and learn to grow from a seemingly negative situation. Then we can grow, learn, or act properly. The bottom line is that people have so much fear because they have such a small amount of faith in God. They really do not believe that God loves them and that God wants to facilitate them. They do not realize their own essence, which is in connection with the Supreme Lord. Therefore, they do not act according to their real identity.

Although the mature devotee understands that the material world is full of miseries and danger at every step, *padam*

padam yad vipadam na tesam, he is *dhira,* very grave, and *akuto-bhayam* or doubtless and fearless. The devotee knows that God is all love and everything is resting on Him.

mattah parataram nanyat
kincid asti dhananjaya
mayi sarvam idam protam
sutre mani-gana iva

O conqueror of wealth, there is no truth superior to Me. Everything rests upon Me, as pearls are strung on a thread.
Bhagavad-gita 7.7

Question: You stated that some people have a fear of giving their hearts because they do not want to risk a broken heart, but they then miss the adventure of deep relationships. In one sense, this seems to be a very rational fear because in this temporary material world, no situation or relationship will permanently last. Any relationship that we have with another conditioned soul will ultimately have to end. Even if it lasts throughout an entire lifetime, death will finally break the connection. On the spiritual level and in the spiritual world, we understand that relationships last eternally with God and His servants, but in the material world, it is inevitably temporary. Consequently, why shouldn't we have a fear of giving our hearts to other conditioned souls who can never fully reciprocate due to their limitations under the modes of material nature?

Answer: Imagine someone asking you, "Why do you worry so much about your young daughter's primary education and needs? In ten years she will be an adolescent and, soon after, an adult. Therefore, what need is there to worry about her particular present needs? Imagine someone then telling you, "You also do not need to give her so much love because in the future she will go off to college, get married, and leave you." Although these are valid concerns, you still see a natural need to do your part. How can your daughter become a healthy adolescent or a mature woman if she is not given the proper facilitation in her earlier years? Although she will later leave the house and will have an even greater love for her husband than for you, you see this as natural. You still see yourself connected to her by the previous affection and care that you offered and still feel capable of continually sending your love.

We know that there are some individuals within spiritual communities who eagerly say that no real love exists in the material world and that we can only have love in heaven, paradise, or in the spiritual world. Such people are only thinking about living in the distant future, but they are unaware that the future is the ever-unfolding present. It is what we do in the present that determines the reality of our real futures. The present is actually the training ground for the future.

Yes, it is true that the most mature experiences of love, which are eternal, are not normally accessible in the material world. However, this does not mean that we should deny our ability to be as loving as we can right now. It is true that the little girl will grow into adolescence and adulthood, and later even leave the house, but it is not proper for the mother to consequently be harsh, insensitive, or impersonal. If she treats her daughter in such a way presently, the future and end results will be devastating.

We all need to love deeply, and we all need to be loved deeply. We need this in order to be a whole person. I refer you to my book, *Spiritual Warrior II*, in which I discuss transforming lust into love. When we address this concept, we are not just talking about lust or Hollywood romance, but we are focusing on selfless, unconditional, divine love, which inevitably must be God-centered. There are many people making the spiritual quest who have become emotionally dry. This is also one reason why some of those in the renounced orders are found to engage in illicit activities and later might even renounce their renunciation for an emotional connection. There are other renunciates who have suppressed their emotions and who deny loving experiences and exchanges but have not transformed the lust. Consequently, the lust may come out in other perverted ways such as false ego, excessive autocracy, harshness, abuse, and exploitation. Some people are slow to give their hearts because they have low self-esteem. One should always feel worthy of being loved and should be alive and fully able to reciprocate.

People who are afraid of giving their hearts because they do not want to risk a broken heart already have a broken heart. We should therefore get out of the broken heart business. Not only do we know people who obviously have broken hearts, but we also know people who are in denial of their severely broken hearts. They are in denial of their emotions and also of their present sadness and pains. Another duty of the spiritual warrior is to recognize those who are emotionally shut down and to help them become transcendentally alive. His or her duty is to help those who are in so much overt chronic fear, sadness, and pain embrace the authentic antidote of love.

Chapter 3

Managing Anger

yenopasrstat purusal
loka udvijate bhrsam
na budhas tad-vasam gacched
icchann abhayam atmanah

A person who desires liberation from
this material world should not fall
under the control of anger because
when bewildered by anger one becomes
a source of dread for all others.
Srimad-Bhagavatam 4.11.32

The Pervasiveness of Anger

Along with fear and anxiety, we will also see an increase in *krodha* or anger as we enter into the twenty-first century. All over the planet, rage is accelerating and manifesting as executive rage, sports rage, airplane rage, and especially road rage. Even ordinary people in seemingly modern countries do not feel comfortable due to fear and paranoia, which constantly keeps them attentive and alert. Such negativity will continue to escalate in the coming decades as the *maya* element increases and as seemingly stable support systems fall apart. As people's relationships break down and they fight more in their material and spiritual environments, people will become even more faithless. After spending many years on a spiritual path and not achieving any of the results due to their own improper practices, some people will even revert back to past bad habits. Some of you, dear readers, may even end up this way if you do not act cautiously.

Therefore, as we embark on this topic, we should take the time to ask ourselves if we have an anger problem or if we feel unable to deal with our anger. We might discover that we do in fact have a problem with anger that we simply cannot recognize. As I began this reflection on anger, I looked at myself in order to see how I handle this emotion. Although I try to think and speak lovingly, I realized that I sometimes have an issue with anger. For those of you who feel that you do not have a problem with anger, you may want to look deeper at the subtle manifestations. The symptoms of such a problem can manifest as a lack of forgiveness or even as a physical sickness. If we constantly carry around such intense frustration, that energy will then affect the body in negative ways.

Anger has different ways of manifesting. In many places at

this time on the planet, people are not only
they are even taking their own lives. Anger al
Both homicide and suicide result from ang
expressions. Suicide and depression are sometimes expressions of anger that people have within themselves. Depression
often stems from some anxiety, disappointment, or loss that
people direct inward, but anger can also manifest externally as
a violent physical or verbal attack. People may even vent their
anger against God or the theists who represent a spiritual com-
mission. Some people engage in ecocide and literally destroy
the natural resources given by Krishna. This violent behavior
is often an expression of anger wrought by people, communities, or nations who have lost control. It often ends in wars and
even with genocide in which one ethnic group tries to destroy
another.

Actually, the real war begins within ourselves. If we cannot
balance our own consciousness, this unsteadiness will surely
manifest in our social environment and in the way we perceive
the world. By recognizing fear and anger as our enemies, we
will have a greater chance to either avoid those enemies or
reduce the effectiveness of their attacks. If we cannot fully
avoid the enemy, we want to at least find ways to lessen its
effect on us so that we will not turn into casualties or unnecessarily slow down our progress. We want to function with
caution because the enemy's camp can dominate us to such an
extent that it can influence all of our interactions.

The Battlefield

In this *Spiritual Warrior* series, we recognize our consciousness to be the battlefield and our weapons to be genuine

knowledge, integrity, compassion, and love. We need these weapons in order to protect ourselves and develop healthy, progressive associations. Otherwise, people's minds will continue to overwhelm them due to the tremendous, negative mental culture on this planet. Unless people have stronger *sadhana* and devotion, they will become causalities. Some of you can already see how your minds go through amazing shifts just from day to day. Sometimes we cannot even find a distinct reason in the environment but it happens due to a lack of proper internal fortification. Through these discussions, we want to look at ways to openly embrace spiritual life with much more zeal and enthusiasm, which naturally happens as we unfold and really see the depths of some of these issues.

Most of the reasons that we take shelter of anger are unhealthy, and although we will mainly address the disadvantages of anger, we will also look at the different aspects of healthy and transcendental anger at the end. We want to share these social, psychological, and spiritual aspects of anger in order to help you become leaders and facilitators.

Why Does Anger Develop

Anger basically results from all of the other enemies of the mind. Enemies such as envy, greed, madness, illusion, fear, and especially lust all lead to anger, which sometimes manifests in very unhealthy ways. In the third chapter of the *Bhagavad-gita*, the Lord describes the cause of anger in His response to one of Arjuna's questions:

arjuna uvaca
atha kena prayukto 'yam
papam carati purusah

anicchann api varsneya
balad iva niyojitah

Arjuna said: O descendant of Vrsni, by
what is one impelled to sinful acts, even
unwillingly, as if engaged by force?

sri-bhagavan uvaca
kama esa krodha esa
rajo-guna-samudbhavah
mahasano maha-papma
viddhy enam iha vairinam

The Supreme Personality of Godhead
said: It is lust only, Arjuna, which is
born of contact with the material mode
of passion and later transformed into
wrath, and which is the all-devouring
sinful enemy of this world.
Bhagavad-gita 3.36-37

Underlying all of the enemies of the mind, we will find lust
or simply misdirected love. Anger also deals with the Rudra
principle, which relates to Lord Siva, a demigod known for his
passion and destructive power. We sometimes even refer to it
as the Ravana principle since it relates to a *raksasa* or demonic
mentality, which vehemently opposes God and spirituality. This
principle of chaos acts as a source of destruction, annihilation,
or disruption. The scriptures explain that Rudra, another name
for Lord Siva, manifests from Lord Brahma's eyebrows as a
result of anger. Anger usually involves passion, but at times,
ignorance overtakes passion at the grossest level. Anger is the

product of lust, which develops from the mode of passion. The purport to *Srimad-Bhagavatam* 3.12.11 states:

> The creation of Rudra from between the eyebrows of Brahma as the result of his anger, generated from the mode of passion partly touched by ignorance, is very significant. In *Bhagavad-gita* 3.37 the principle of Rudra is described. *Krodha* (anger) is the product of *kama* (lust), which is the result of the mode of passion. When lust and hankering are unsatisfied, the element of *krodha* appears, which is the formidable enemy of the conditioned soul. The most sinful and inimical passion is represented as *ahankara*, or the false egocentric attitude of thinking oneself to be all in all. Such an egocentric attitude on the part of the conditioned soul, who is completely under the control of material nature, is described in *Bhagavad-gita* as foolish. The egocentric attitude is a manifestation of the Rudra principle in the heart, wherein *krodha* (anger) is generated. This anger develops in the heart and is further manifested through various senses, like the eyes, hands and legs. When a man is angry he expresses such anger with red-hot eyes and sometimes makes a display of clenching his fists or

kicking his legs. This exhibition of the Rudra principle is the proof of Rudra's presence in such places. When a man is angry he breathes very rapidly, and thus Rudra is represented in the air of life, or in the activities of breathing. When the sky is overcast with dense clouds and roars in anger, and when the wind blows very fiercely, the Rudra principle is manifested, and so also when the seawater is infuriated by the wind it appears in a gloomy feature of Rudra, which is very fearful to the common man. When fire is ablaze we can also experience the presence of Rudra, and when there is an inundation over the earth we can understand that this is also the representation of Rudra.

Srimad-Bhagavatam 3.12.11, purport

This purport shows how these moods of chaos and great passion form a part of the Rudra principle. Passion is the activity responsible for creation, chaos, and destruction. This energetic expression is covered with lust and projected according to *ahankara* or false ego. These disturbances are like unhealthy friends who come to associate very closely with us. The enemies such as lust, anger, and greed support each other in various coalitions and sometimes they all attack at the same time in a very vehement and aggressive mood. This occurs when lust and hankering are unsatisfied. When we develop genuine detachment, we do not hanker to that extent.

Myths about Anger

A Biological Myth

People have many myths about anger that cause them to categorize the issue in a certain way. For instance, some people consider anger to be biological or hereditary, but this myth does not have any solid foundation. Although some people are more prone to anger due to their psychophysical make-up or emersion in the modes of passion and ignorance, their socialization or quality of association will have a greater impact on their reactions. Although we do bring forth other influences into a situation such as our *karma*, which affects the ways in which we respond to specific situations, it is a myth that anger is biological and a permanent, unchangeable aspect of the body.

The Futility of Sense Indulgence

It is also a myth that venting our anger will help us deal with it. Some therapists and spiritual systems instruct people to fully express their anger in order to release the feeling. Next to their meditation room, some therapists might have a room in which people can beat punching bags, scream, kick, and cry. If someone has a problem with their husband, wife, or mother-in-law, they might express their anger by beating a pillow that they visualize as the person. Some psychiatrists actually consider this to be a healthy release of anger.

However, if people could become more whole and spiritual just by acting upon their sense gratification, then we should accept the pig or other similar species as the most evolved because they do not have any sense of restriction. Actually, the more we feed certain emotions or even addictions, the more we will receive the same negative reactions. The more we act upon our irrational mood of anger, the more we integrate it into our existence. The more a person overeats, oversleeps, or engages in excessive sex, the more he or she will become habituated to such activities. Even in terms of drugs, the more we take, the more we need to feel the same relief from the pain.

The expression of anger alone does not cause the relief. Actually, since anger relates extensively to the element of stress, a physical expression may in fact relieve some of the tension but not always. The stress will usually still remain and it will come out again in some other situation. Whether we project the anger onto the actual person or substitute the anger, it will just reinforce the emotion or cause it to increase.

Triggers of Anger

In this section, we want to examine which expressions, thoughts, or actions trigger our anger. This relates to what we will call "shoulds" and "blamers" which all lead to anger. The main problem is that anger leads to more anger and violence leads to more violence. Another person may not see a situation in the same way or may not even understand that they have hurt us. Even if they did consciously try to hurt us, we will not help solve the issue by coming down to their same level. To degrade or dehumanize ourselves in this way will only bring defeat and weakness in spiritual life. We will allow another person's weaknesses or *anarthas* to dictate our life since the past will preoccupy our present and future. It will drain us of our spiritual strength and power.

Five "Shoulds"
1. **"Since I have a desire, other people should respond to my desire."** We can easily recognize the inherent prob-

lem with this mentality. First of all, other people also have their own desires, which may not always harmonize with our own. In order to rectify this unhealthy tendency, we need to abandon selfishness, value other people more, and become more reflective.

2. **"Since I have a certain idea or standard, other people should also have the same exact one."** If someone strays from our standard, we may resort to anger. It all depends on our mentality. We often think that others should have the same mentality or code of ethics even though their situations may differ from our own.

3. **"If a problem develops, the other person should change."** When problems arise, we sometimes want the other person to change instead of us. If the other person does not change and we adamantly maintain our mindset, we will again develop anger. We need to recognize that their perceptions, *karma*, or realizations may completely differ from our own. The other person may in fact want to change, but we also need to acknowledge that he or she may not feel a need to change due to their situation.

4. **"If you love me and care for me, you should do X, Y, and Z."** This "should" depends on an assumption. The result that we expect depends on an assumed reality that we have about how the other person thinks which will automatically dictate their actions.

5. **"Since you have hurt me and I feel hurt, I should take revenge."** Due to some negative interaction in a relationship, one person may want to hurt the other person in return, which is obviously unhealthy.

Four "Blamers"

1. **"When we see everything in black and white, we will blame another person if something strays from our narrow vision."** Many people have an extremely narrow vision. They do not try to understand the essence or some of the important mitigating factors of a situation. Consequently, they quickly become disturbed if something does not fit into their limited evaluations and perspectives.

2. **"When we think that we understand the mind of another person, we will put labels on him and even blame him if he does not act according to those labels."** When people try to read the mind of another person, they will naturally become angry when he or she does not act accordingly. We can see the inherent problems in this practice because, unless a person has some unusual psychic powers, he or she will usually make incorrect assumptions. The other person's thoughts may even directly oppose the assumption.

3. **"If a person disturbs us, we exaggerate by making extreme generalizations that cover over the whole relationship."** For instance, a person might claim, "This always happens. You always act in the same way." Although the incident may have only happened once or twice, we allow our whole perception of the situation to change. We exaggerate the situation with the words "always" and "never" which now causes us to overreact in an irate type of mood. "Blamers" always blame the other person.

4. **"Due to a behavior that we do not appreciate, we now attach a label onto another person and categorize the person according to that label."** For example, you may label a person as a jerk, imbecile, moron, or fool, and this label will influence your entire perception of them. Even if they act in admirable ways, due to this label, your anger will overpower the relationship or the moment.

Nine Positive Ways to Deal with "Shoulds" and "Blamers"

1. **Avoid self-centeredness or selfishness.** By abandoning our own selfishness, we will find it much easier to understand someone else's viewpoint or position. It will help us understand their actions, pain, hurt, or needs. It is not just a matter of being right; rather, it is a matter of producing a loving effect. A genuine spiritualist never just wants to be right. Actually, a person with this mindset is a *jnani* or philosopher who will never reach a deep level of *bhakti* or devotion. We want to be right in the right way so that we can constantly honor, embrace, and glorify God.

2. **Avoid assumptions when we judge.** The mind is so wild and prone to all kinds of speculation. Consequently, we must be careful before we jump to prejudiced conclusions.

3. **First change ourselves so that we can help affect others.** We can think, "What changes do I need to make in my own life so that I can encourage that change in someone else." It means that we need to stop minimizing our own potency and stop blaming others. Although another

person may have real issues, we still have our own ability to make a difference because God has no favorites. He is in everyone's heart. Everyone has the ability to influence their environment if they recognize their eternal identity as divine entities.

4. **Try to understand the environment more closely.** By closely studying the field of activities, one can gain a better understanding of cause and effect, which will decrease the likelihood of an overreaction.

5. **Revenge will only compound a problem rather than resolve it.** Revenge will just drag us down to the other person's level, hinder us from acting productively, and cause us to constantly live in the past. All of us have acted in unbeneficial ways in the past and we hope that others will forgive us. We forgive so that we can also be forgiven. We also forgive for ourselves because we want to constantly access love.

6. **Always look for the deeper meaning in any situation.** We do not just want to embrace the immediate, irrational expression of anger, especially since the first emotional impression can be very misleading and superficial.

7. **Ask questions to get healthier feedback.** Good questions can give us more facts and much more insight, sympathy, and empathy.

8. **Be realistic and honest when dealing with issues.** In this way, all parties will know how to authentically deal with the conflict. If parties are not revealing their real fears,

anxieties, and needs, the conflict will not be resolved and can even escalate.

9. **Value other people more.** If we can develop a deeper level of appreciation, whatever happens in their lives will become important to us and will help us find a way to glorify God more. If we do not value others, it will be hard to have authentic, healthy, and meaningful relationships.

The Progression of Anger

An Adverse Chain Reaction

As anger escalates, it progresses through certain steps. Mundane anger usually manifests in an adverse chain of intense verbal expressions, gestures, and mannerisms. If we see this chain of events unfolding, we may need to act with caution because we do not want to submerge ourselves in this negativity. We can also try to help the other person avoid this intensity.

If we completely lose control of the anger, we may act so destructively within a relationship that it will later require more time, energy, and resources to rectify the problem and rebuild the relationship. We can avoid all this trouble simply by honoring and addressing the situation properly from the very beginning. Then we will feel happier in our lives and have the ability to give more value to others. We will develop spirituality in a very dynamic way. The following techniques can help us recognize anger when it begins to escalate.

Techniques to Recognize the Progression of Anger

1. **Check the habit of mind reading.** Mind reading happens

when one person speculates about the thoughts of another person, accepts this speculation as true, and then acts on the speculation. We can stop this by taking more time to understand the person's real intentions and concerns.

2. **Implement time-out in negative situations.** For instance, if a situation simply turns into a combative conflict, we could say, "Maybe we should finish this conversation tomorrow or this evening." In this way, we will have a greater chance to address the conflict in a rational way and to access a loving connection rather than an unhealthy, emotional one.

This technique can help some of you as you deal with your children. If their behavior leads you to feel irrational anger, it might help to punish them at a later time when you can address the behavior in a more rational manner. You let them know that you disapprove of their actions, but you give them the chastisement at a time when you have more control over your anger. In this way, the chastisement will proportionately correspond to the issue so that it will bring rectification instead of an assault or devastation.

Time-out will give us a chance to read, chant, pray, or meditate which will remind us about the purpose of the relationship and about our real identity. Most importantly, it will give us an opportunity to give more care and love. We do not simply want to prove the other person wrong and take revenge through retaliation. Even after reflecting on the situation, we may still conclude that the other person has acted improperly; however, now that we have come to a healthy understanding, we can try to facilitate in a positive way.

3. **Monitor our self-talk.** Self-talk refers to the positive or negative things that we tell ourselves, and for the average person, studies indicate that the majority of thoughts are negative. Many people focus solely on their weaknesses and the reasons for such weaknesses. They meditate on the people who anger them and the reasons for their anger. The list goes on and on. For this reason, it is very important to acknowledge the power of the mind, which can be our greatest enemy. If we do not check such negativity, these harmful messages will control us.

4. **Write verses or notes on a set of cards that we can access in urgent situations.** In this way, when we find ourselves overwhelmed by our emotions, we can try to review one of the cards describing the proper way to act in a certain situation. We can record many different prayers or spiritual perspectives to help us under all types of circumstances.

5. **Practice proper behavior through visualizations.** For example, if you have a problematic relationship, you can visualize your next interaction with the person and visualize a positive response to their behavior. In this way, you can try to change past patterns that have negated the love factor and resulted in anger. You will bring with you a great sense of strength and clarity when you move into the person's physical presence. Athletes as well as expert businessmen practice this technique. They already have a vision for the future in the present; therefore, the present turns into an organized and controlled reality since their minds have already embraced the proper course of action.

6. **Practice rehearsing our behaviors in the mirror or with another person.** In this way, we will have more control of ourselves and bring forth more love.

7. **Try to channel the negative energy because lust is ultimately misdirected love.** We do not just want to repress or deny the energy, but we can try to channel it into constructive, creative, and healthy engagements. Sometimes the greatest creations have come out of anxieties. Some of the greatest prayers, meditations, poems, or literatures have developed from that energy which the person then channels into a productive expression.

8. **Negotiate and explain need in a palatable way so that all sides can genuinely communicate and develop appreciation.** It will also help us to become more aware of the science of mediation and conflict resolution. This will definitely help a person to understand and control their own as well as others' anger.

Effects of Anger

Physical Problems
Anger has many consequences, including physiological effects. For instance, researchers involved law students in a study that lasted over a period of twenty-five years. Out of the 118 attorneys who had taken the Minnesota Multiphasic Personality Inventory twenty-five years earlier as law students, those who had scored in the upper quartile on the hostility scale were 4.2 times more likely to die prematurely. In another study, researchers also recognized that the more hostile Type A

person might have greater rates of heart disease due to the frequent and potentially damaging hormones released during the fight-or-flight response.[8] This basically means that people who suffer from excessive anger and aggression are more likely to have a premature death. From this study, we can see the effects on one's physical existence. We also know that anger leads to hypertension, ulcers, and hardening of the arteries along with many other ailments.

Social Disturbances

From a sociological perspective, people gradually begin to avoid a person who constantly exhibits anger. Even if such a person has something of value to share, others will be less likely to accept it due to their fury. It will hinder their ability to communicate with others and express their particular needs. However, an angry person may sometimes even get what they want just because other people will react to their anger to pacify them. In one sense, anger is a sign of need, but if it is expressed with violence or with unhealthy words, it can cause the opposite effect. It may cause others to shut down rather than to reciprocate or assist. If we deeply look at our own anger, we will see that it often creates the opposite of what we really want.

Spiritual Weaknesses and Offenses

Unfortunately, the spiritual costs of anger are even higher. It can lead to all types of offenses such as offenses to devotees, the holy name, the holy places of pilgrimage as well as to the spiritual master. Not only can anger cause us to offend the devotees and the spiritual master, but it can also cause us to execute our services in a ridiculous way. Anger is comparable to spiritual suicide.

In the Fourth Canto of the *Srimad-Bhagavatam*, Daksa, one of the demigods, exhibits irrational and misplaced anger, which cannot be checked even by good advice and encouragement. The anger completely bewilders his intelligence. If we fall prey to this unhealthy aspect of anger, we will lose our clarity of vision and our proper perspective, which can devastate us spiritually. In the *Srimad-Bhagavatam* 4.2.19, Daksa actually curses Lord Siva due to anger:

> *nisidhyamanah sa sadasya-mukhyair*
> *dakso giritraya visrjya sapam*
> *tasmad viniskramy vivrddha-manyur*
> *jagama kauravya nijam niketanam*

> Maitreya continued: My dear Vidura, in spite of the requests of all the members of the sacrificial assembly, Daksa, in great anger, cursed Lord Siva and then left the assembly and went back to his home.

Srila Prabhupada writes in his purport:

> Anger is so detrimental that even a great personality like Daksa, out of anger, left the arena where Brahma was presiding and all the great sages and pious and saintly persons were assembled. All of them requested him not to leave, but, infuriated, he left, thinking that the auspicious place was not fit for him. Puffed up by his exalted

position, he thought that no one was greater than he in argument. It appears that all the members of the assembly, including Lord Brahma, requested him not to be angry and leave their company, but in spite of all these requests, he left. That is the effect of cruel anger. In *Bhagavad-gita*, therefore, it is advised that one who desires to make tangible advancement in spiritual consciousness must avoid three things—lust, anger and the mode of passion. Actually we can see that lust, anger and passion make a man crazy, even though he be as great as Daksa. The very name Daksa suggests that he was expert in all material activities, but still, because of his aversion towards such a saintly personality as Siva, he was attacked by these three enemies—anger, lust and passion. Lord Caitanya, therefore, advised that one be very careful not to offend Vaisnavas. He compared offenses toward a Vaisnava to a mad elephant. As a mad elephant can do anything horrible, so when a person offends a Vaisnava he can perform any abominable action.

The *Bhagavad-gita* tells us that attachment leads to illusion and then to bewilderment and fall down. In this case, many great sages or *rsis* tried to instruct Daksa, but his anger had bewildered his intelligence to such an extent that he could not recognize his own improper behavior or hear from others. We must avoid these negative tendencies if we want to make advancement. It is not optional. Any time we see excessive lust or anger emerging in our consciousness, we should recognize it as a warning. It will disturb our ability to enter into the divine relationship in the spiritual kingdom under the service of the Divine Couple or Mother-Father God.

Lust, anger, and passion make people crazy and, in devotional circles as well as in material circles, people can act in horrible ways due to anger although they will usually regret such abominable actions later. Often people will hurt their closest associates instead of giving them love. In this case, Daksa should have had great love and appreciation for his son-in-law, Lord Siva, along with all the other great personalities such as Lord Brahma. However, due to his intense irritation, he could not hear any rational instructions from this great assembly of sages who, in unison, attempted to instruct him.

Conceals the Cause of the Pain

Anger can cause us to hide or conceal our pains if we use it as a defense mechanism. Sometimes the expression of anger may manifest from loneliness, fear, guilt, hurt, or even pride. Although these feelings may externally appear as anger, we will find a much deeper cause. Pride especially has adverse effects. If *yogis* and *panditas* or scholars lack sufficient devotion in spite of their austerities and penances, instead of developing love and compassion, they will simply develop knowledge, power, and even anger. This is a very subtle aspect of anger that sometimes manifests among great *yogis* who might even curse each other. Daksa's behavior exhibits this negative reaction. First he cursed Lord Siva, and Nandisvara, one of Lord

Siva's principal associates, later cursed all the supporters of Daksa. Finally, the sage Bhrgu condemned all the followers of Lord Siva with another very strong curse. The situation turned into a complete mess. All of these *brahmanas* had power and *sakti*, but due to the lack of *bhakti* in some cases, the illusion covered over their knowledge.

Creates Irrational Responses to Situations

Anger may also disturb us by causing a situation to affect us on a much larger scale than necessary. For instance, if someone's actions or words disturbed us, we may now allow a cloud to cover the way in which we see and deal with that person. Repressed anger can also lead to irrational reflections, which cause us to act accordingly or hinder our ability to function properly. Sometimes we might even have a genuine reason to feel anger, but instead of giving it an excessive amount of attention, we can try to separate the activity from the person. We hear, "Hate the sin but not the sinner." Although a person may sin, we should always have a certain level of appreciation and affection for him or her. When a genuine issue disturbs us, we can still feel uncomfortable about the activity without attaching a label too directly onto the person.

We do not want to incorporate our anger about a specific negative action into all of our interactions with the person. Such a mindset is unhealthy even if it just lasts for a moment. We do not have to turn the incident into a protracted issue. If another person has acted in a displeasing way, as caring individuals, we still have the responsibility to respond with integrity, thoughtfulness, and compassion. However, if that response involves labeling the individual rather than taking thoughtful action, it takes away from unconditional love. It takes away our ability to serve as a genuine caretaker and help the other person.

Anger Management

Counteracting Negativity

Anger management is an essential technology for the spiritual warrior. We should not minimize the serious effects of anger, which lead to violence and even wars. Some of the terrorists feel so much anger that they will even take their own lives in order to hurt someone else. Obviously, this intense anger will only increase in a society in which people feel lonely, unprotected, and threatened. As a reaction to these attacks and threats, people tend to strike out in self-defense.

Furthermore, when people feel that others do not value them or their needs, the culture of anger will also proportionately grow. Although this negative culture will continuously increase, the spiritualist has the duty to try to counteract its influence and facilitate the victims. If possible, spiritualists should first try to weed out these enemies in their own consciousness and then act as spiritual warriors to assist others. We want to look at this issue from many different angles so that people can first help themselves and then help others.

Keep a Journal

Journaling is one technique that can help us manage our anger. Writing often helps us look deeper into the issues in our lives. It can also help us increase our level of accountability because, when we do not plan or strategize, *maya* or illusion will plan for us. We can either make plans to accelerate in our devotion or we can allow the duality of *martya-loka* or the planet of death to completely bombard us with relative or transitory concerns. If we succumb to the influence of our environment, the senses and the mind will literally drag us away:

mamaivamso jiva-loke
jiva-bhutah sanatanah
manah-sasthanindriyani
prakrti-sthani karsati

The living entities in this conditioned world are My eternal fragmental parts. Due to conditioned life, they are struggling very hard with the six senses, which include the mind.

Bhagavad-gita 15.7

The mind causes intense suffering as it responds to the senses in unhealthy ways.

In our journals, we can monitor our level of anger by using a scale from 1-10. On a particular day, we can use a number on this scale to rate our level of aggression and our level of arousal. In this way, we can monitor our emotions daily and also try to pinpoint which situations excite our anger or cause us to lose control. By constantly observing ourselves, we can find ways to incite love rather than lust because lust always stems from excessive attachments or overreactions.

Evaluate the Experience

In order to manage anger, we can also try to **name it, face it, feel it, and release it**. We must first identify the enemy before it discreetly sneaks into the environment. If it successfully enters our arena, it will cause all types of destruction like a cancer or time bomb. Many people live in a state of constant crisis and, as a result, they cannot experience deeper levels of love and realization. Due to the anger, which may stem from negative experiences in the past, they generalize those experi-

ences and then carry this mentality into their rel
others. Consequently, it interferes with their ab
present in their interactions with other people and in their ability to say "yes" to God at every moment. We can look at our
day and evaluate our experiences in order to discover which
situations trigger our anger so that we can deal with it accordingly.

Stress Relievers

We all know that certain basic activities relieve stress
such as exercise, meditation, visualizations, and affirmations. Exercise releases positive stimulating hormones, which
change the brain chemistry and strengthen the immune system.
Meditation, visualizations, and affirmations can all distinctly
bring about a relaxation response and can help one focus more
intensely on healthy reflections and actions. These stress reduction techniques can help us check our anger, especially when
we go deeper into our spiritual activities. However, when our
problems are very chronic, we will need additional technologies that can create penetrating and lasting results.

Abandon Hypocrisy through Genuine
Spiritual Practices

As we become more introspective through chanting or
meditation, the conscious mind will gradually calm down.
However, if we do not allow ourselves to really embrace the
mantra or transcendental sound vibration while we chant or
pray, we will not derive the full benefit. For instance, if a person
gives to a charity but gives in an angry mood, the act will not
have the same positive effect. Although the holy name of God
and the nine-fold process are very powerful, if we constantly
commit offenses, we will not receive the full value or potency.

Spiritual Warrior IV

This issue affects Vaisnava communities all over the world and even other religious traditions. Although people have bona fide scriptures and teachers, hypocrisy often overrules genuine performance. Hypocrisy on the part of both leaders and followers is often more dominant than genuine, authentic devotion and realizations. All over we see an increase in churches, mosques, and temples, but the national and international problems in the world order continue to increase. The problems have escalated to such an extent that some of the greatest assaults against humanity stem from religion itself. Fanaticism is one of these serious assaults that manifests from so-called religion. The current situation on the planet is not quite right. We need more open communication and the ability to authentically look at ourselves and others. We need to raise our own standards so that we can genuinely care for other people and give them more of ourselves. By raising our own standards, we will be able to present ourselves much more effectively due to our own purity.

Understanding the Essence

We want to look closer at the scriptures in order to gain more insight. It is often important to turn to the scriptures and allow them to come alive. Sometimes spiritualists have so much knowledge but still do not have the ability to change unhealthy patterns in their lives. For this reason, we find that some spiritualists also go to therapists, suffer from depression, and even commit suicide. If a good therapist can understand the client's philosophy and genuine needs, he or she can help the client remove many blocks. In this way, the spiritualist can more holistically embrace their own philosophy and increase their authenticity and productivity in many areas.

Sometimes we need to look closer at what transpires in our mind and consciousness so that we can let Krishna or God in much more. We want to take advantage of the opportunity to address these issues because, in spite of all of the philosophies and spiritual paths in this age of Kali, most people still do not understand the essence. What does this mean? Do the processes given to us by the great *acaryas* or the prophets lack potency? No. People lack the potency to really understand their essence. Due to the excessive misery on the planet, spiritualists need to be genuine and fully authentic in order to assist in raising the level of consciousness. They need to be proactive instead of reactive and whole within themselves in order to more effectively help others.

In the *Bhagavad-gita* 15.15, the Lord says:

> *sarvasya caham hrdi sannivisto*
> *mattah smrtir jnanam apohanam ca*

> I am seated in everyone's heart,
> and from Me come remembrance,
> knowledge and forgetfulness.

Krishna is hiding in the heart, waiting for the opportunity to come forth and give full cognizance, full love, and full association. However, if anger and lust permeate our hearts, they will cover Krishna's wonderful presence as *paramatma*, the Lord in the heart, and prevent the realization and guidance from entering into our consciousness.

The contents of the heart will obviously affect the mind and gradually manifest in our words and actions. Of course, in the process of *sadhana-bhakti* or devotional service in practice, we involve all of our senses in God's service. If these enemies capture our senses, we will not be able to properly engage them in Krishna's service. If we cannot even employ our senses properly, we will not move from the basic level of fundamental devotional service. We will not develop real *ruci* (spiritual taste) or *prema* (love) because we will preoccupy our existence with the mundane. Anger is a great enemy because it harasses and incarcerates the *bhakti-lata-bija* or the devotional creeper. We want to break these shackles that interfere with the creeper.

Tiny Puddles of Anger

The purport of *Srimad-Bhagavatam* 11.4.11 explains:

> Those who do not accept the devotional service of the Supreme Lord can be considered in two categories. Those engaged in sense gratification are easily conquered by the demigods through various weapons such as hunger, thirst, sexual desire, lamentation for the past and vain hoping for the future. Such materialistic fools, infatuated with the material world, are easily controlled by the demigods, who are the ultimate supplying agents of sense gratification. But according to Sridhara Swami, persons who attempt to subdue the desires of the material senses and thus avoid the control of the demigods

without surrendering to the Supreme
Lord are even more foolish than the
sense gratifiers. Although crossing
the ocean of sense gratification, those
who perform severe penances without
service to the Lord eventually drown
in tiny puddles of anger. One who
simply performs material penances
does not actually purify his heart. By
one's material determination one may
restrict the activities of the senses
although one's heart is still filled with
material desires. The practical result
of this is *krodha*, or anger. We have
seen artificial performers of penance
who have become very bitter and angry
through denial of the senses.

In spite of extreme austerities and penances, if one
lacks *bhakti*, one will access anger in a more intense mood
because one will have more mystic powers to use as weapons.
Sometimes people engage in scriptural arguments, but since
they do not have a devotional consciousness, they simply beat
each other over the head with the scriptures.

Healthy Anger

Anger as a Catalyst
Beyond the unhealthy aspects of anger, we will find some
healthy and even transcendental aspects of anger. In one sense,
anger is easily recognizable because it is a part of life. It is a

reaction or an overreaction to a situation. However, we must always ask, "How do we use anger for growth and acceleration back into our original consciousness?"

Anger can function as a distinct catalyst that helps us look closer at ourselves and at the situation. If we find ourselves in a situation that makes us angry, we can look at the cause of the anger, which may not even relate to the specific person. This intense introspection can help us find a more positive resolution. Sometimes anger gives us a chance to look at our own selfishness. It helps us see our own desires so that we can determine where they stem from and where they want to go.

Once again, anger can act as a barometer so that we can step back and look at the situation from a proper perspective. Martin Luther King used anger productively instead of destructively because his anger against the discrimination toward African-Americans pushed him to act in a positive way. In this case, his anger began a powerful movement towards change. In some cases, anger can activate a person to act positively. Mahatma Gandhi also used his anger to create a powerful nonviolent movement to demand India's independence from the British.

On the material level, if someone physically attacks you, anger can even engender strength, fortitude, and determination. If someone crosses healthy boundaries in a relationship, anger can help you remain conscientious about the situation. For instance, if someone touches a person in the wrong place, a strong response will clearly indicate that the person will not tolerate such behavior. It does not have to be a violent retaliation, but the person can clearly establish his or her own boundaries. Of course, it provides a chance to look at the deeper issues within ourselves. We also recognize anger as a natural stage in the grieving process, which we will discuss in more depth in the next chapter. Before one can entirely resolve the grief, one

normally experiences a period of anger as
and deal with the issue.

Spiritual Application of Anger

Anger definitely has some healthy purposes in the spiritual sense. For instance, although blasphemy disturbs us, we should not just feel anger but also compassion and concern for the blasphemer. People who make such offenses actually commit more of an injustice to themselves. A spiritualist should feel compassion for such an offender because the person might seriously damage his or her own spiritual growth and devotional creeper. We could consider the spiritualist's intense feelings to be a type of anger. Actually, he feels deep compassion for the offender because such actions or words will only lead to degradation.

The actions of Maharaja Prthu as described in the *Srimad-Bhagavatam* exemplify healthy anger. At one point, Maharaja Prthu became very angry because the citizens came to him in a rather unfortunate state. In this state of deprivation, they appealed to the king since he has the duty to provide protection. As they approached him with thin bodies due to a lack of food, he was very alert and attentive to their feelings and needs. He was concerned for their well-being, and he wanted to discover the cause of their suffering and bring happiness to those under his jurisdiction. He also showed that leaders should be equally disposed towards all instead of having favorites and they should address problems and deviations when they arise. Therefore, after evaluating the situation, he realized that Mother Earth was responsible and he prepared to take action. In the Fourth Canto of the *Srimad-Bhagavatam*, the great sage Maitreya describes this pastime in detail to Vidura:

maitreya uvaca
yadabhisiktah prthur anga viprair
amantrito janatayas ca palah
praja niranne ksiti-prstha etya
ksut-ksama-dehah patim abhyavocan

The great sage Maitreya continued: My dear Vidura, at the time King Prthu was enthroned by the great sages and *brahmanas* and declared to be the protector of the citizens, there was a scarcity of food grains. The citizens actually became skinny due to starvation. Therefore they came before the King and informed him of their real situation.

vayam rajan jatharenabhitapta
yathagnina kotara-sthena vrksah
tvam adya yatah saranam saranyam
yah sadhito vrtii-karah patir nah
tan no bhavan ihatu ratave 'nnam
ksudharditanam naradeva-deva
yavan na nanksyamaha ujjhitorja
varta-patis tvam kila loka-palah

Dear King, just as a tree with a fire burning in the hollow of the trunk gradually dries up, we are drying up due to the fire of hunger in our stomachs. You are the protector of surrendered souls, and you have been appointed to give employment to us. Therefore we have all come to you for protection. You are not only a king, but the incarnation of God as well. Indeed, you are the king of all kings. You can give us all kinds of occupational engagements, for you are the master of our livelihood. Therefore, O king of all kings, please arrange to satisfy our hunger by the proper distribution of food grains. Please take care of us, lest we should die for want of food.

maitreya uvaca
prthuh prajanam karunam
nisamya paridevitam
dirgham dadhyau kurusrestha
nimittam so 'nvapadyata

After hearing this lamentation and seeing the pitiable condition of the citizens, King Prthu contemplated this matter for a long time to see if he could find out the underlying causes.

iti vyavasito buddhya
pragrhita-sarasanah
sandadhe visikham bhumeh
kruddhas tripura-ha yatha

Having arrived at a conclusion, the King took up his bow and arrow and

aimed them at the earth, exactly like
Lord Siva, who destroys the whole
world out of anger.

pravepamana dharani
nisamyodayudham ca tam
gauh saty apadravad bhita
mrgiva mrgayu-druta

When the earth saw that King Prthu
was taking his bow and arrow to kill
her, she became very much afraid and
began to tremble. She then began to
flee, exactly like a deer, which runs
very swiftly when followed by a hunter.
Being afraid of King Prthu, she took
the shape of a cow and began to run.

tam anvadhavat tad vainyah
kupito 'tyaruneksanah
saram dhanusi sandhaya
yatra yatra palayate

Seeing this, Maharaja Prthu became
very angry, and his eyes became as red
as the early-morning sun. Placing an
arrow on his bow, he chased the cow-
shaped earth wherever she would run.
Srimad-Bhagavatam 4.17.9-15

Hopefully, we will gradually begin to see a distinction
between mundane anger and spiritual or transcendental anger.

Although we see anger in this pastime, Maharaja Prthu did not display irrational anger. He was attentive to the needs of His citizens, and, after scrutinizing the situation, he discovered the cause and went into healthy action. Maharaja Prthu displayed an interesting sequence of healthy anger. After the citizens came to the king with their problem, he immediately took action due to his compassion and his desire to see them happy. He responded to their complaints with an intense focus that the *Bhagavatam* describes as anger. However, the anger came from a natural situation since the Earth withheld the necessary foodstuff. As a leader, he wanted to show that he would not tolerate her behavior and took immediate action. His behavior exemplifies a healthy use of anger.

Foolish Anger

The *Srimad-Bhagavatam* 4.26.22 describes another aspect of healthy anger.

paramo 'nugraho dando
bhrtyesu prabhunarpitah
balo na veda tat tanvi
bandhu-krtyam amarsanah

My dear slender maiden, when a master chastises his servant, the servant should accept this as great mercy. One who becomes angry must be very foolish not to know that such is the duty of his friend.

The purport explains:
It is said that when a foolish man is

instructed in something very nice, he
generally cannot accept it. Indeed, he
actually becomes angry. Such anger is
compared to the poison of a serpent, for
when a serpent is fed milk and bananas,
its poison actually increases. Instead of
becoming merciful or sober, the serpent
increases its poisonous venom when
fed nice foodstuffs. Similarly, when a
fool is instructed, he does not rectify
himself, but actually becomes angry.

Sometimes a person feels angry when the master or parent
chastises him or her out of affection. However, it is healthy for
a parent or master to feel concern for their dependents and to
seemingly express that concern through anger in order to help
their constituents act in beneficial ways. It sometimes requires
intensity to convey that message.

A spiritual master has the right to
chastise his disciple any way He likes.
A *sisya* or a disciple means one who
accepts the disciplinary action given
by the spiritual master. Even though
sometimes a spiritual master chastises
his disciple as a fool or rascal in fatherly
affection, it does not mean necessarily
that the disciple is a fool or a rascal.
You will find even in the statement of
Lord Caitanya—He presents Himself
as a fool designated by His spiritual
master, but that does not mean that He

was a fool. A sincere disciple fee
pleasurable when his spiritual m;
chastises him with calling him
names as fool and rascal.[9]

Mundane Anger Does Not Exist

Anger is a Choice

Just as grief and lamentation do not really exist, anger does
not really exist in a tangible form. It is not a separate entity;
rather, it is a part of the illusion that we create and even feed.
In any situation that causes us to respond with mundane anger,
we have made that particular choice according to our perception. Consequently, we act according to the way in which we
codify a particular interaction. Actually, it really does not exist.
No one has to be weighed down by mundane anger; it is an
individual creation that a person holds, feeds, and allows to
develop and grow. It can cause many physical, psychological,
social, and spiritual disturbances. At every moment, the mind
has the ability to accept or reject. Our desire and the intensity
of our spiritual greed will determine whether we accept and
play into unhealthy reactions. It is just that simple but also that
complex.

We can free our minds by understanding the power that
Krishna has given us or by understanding the purity of our original nature. The nature of the soul is *sac-cid-ananda-vigraha* or
eternal, blissful, and full of knowledge. In our original state, we
are all pure, but since we have accepted the illusion, we allow
ourselves to think differently which then leads to improper
words and actions. Although all of these enemies of the mind

do not really exist, we consider them to be very dominant. As a result, we feed them and create a whole paradigm based on such reflections.

When we encounter situations that produce anger, we have four choices. First, we can take responsibility. For instance, Maharaja Prthu acknowledged the genuine problem, and even though he felt angry, he channeled it in a way that would bring about the best resolution. In this way, he responded positively. Secondly, we can openly communicate our problem because spiritualists should act as the well-wishers of others. We should try to see each other as *prabhu* or master and friend. We should feel the misery of another person as well as their happiness: *param-duhkha-duhkhi-krpam-buddhi*. We want to understand and identify with the struggles of another person as if they were our own. Therefore, we openly negotiate or strategize in order to come to a healthy resolution. Next, we can also choose to separate ourselves from the environment or situation in order to detach ourselves. We can resolve many problems more quickly by trying to view the situation as an outside observer. Finally, sometimes we may even need to remember the *karma* factor in order to maintain a balanced perspective.

Part of the Illusion

Anger is a creation of the illusion, which we feed according to improper or excessive reactions. We have the full ability to stop feeding and identifying with this mundane, unhealthy anger. We have the choice to accept or reject these negative emotions. Spiritual life is not complex or beyond our grasp. We always have a current connection with Krishna, with the spiritual world, and with the great *acaryas*. We always have a connection with *rasa-tattva* or the eternal relationships of the soul. However, we continuously feed into the total material nature along with the three modes. The *maha-tattva* or the total material energy basically deals with people who, in a state of insanity, feed the illusion and construct an entire network around this illusion. Such people go through all types of activities that cause them to suffer.

Anger in God

Some may ask, "Is there anger in God?" Yes, all things are included within the Godhead including anger. Otherwise, where would anger come from? The Lord is the source of everything because He is absolute. His anger is as good as His mercy or any other expression of His mercy. The difference between our anger and transcendental anger is that when we become angry, we normally become disturbed and void of mercy. The Lord's anger and mercy are the same because He is giving great attention to the situation or the person at both times.

The same understanding also applies to the Lord's pure servants. Their anger is actually a benediction because they are always thinking of the Lord and doing everything within their power to glorify Him. Even their anger will push us towards a deeper level of authenticity. On the absolute platform, all emotions are expressions in the service of God. God is good. He is good when He is angry and He is good when He is merciful. Sometimes the Supreme Lord appears in different incarnations, and during some of these pastimes, He is angry at the demons and the sinful. He chastises them as a way to help them eventually come back home to Him. In this mood of chastisement, He sometimes manifests an even greater extension of His love in comparison to the times in which He simply gives love through encouragement and protection.

The Perverted Reflection

If we want to accept the existence of anger, we can accept its reality in the purest sense. We already described healthy anger, which manifests in its purest state. Lamentation and grief also exist in the spiritual world in their perfect state. All of these unhealthy dysfunctional patterns and interactions result from the modes of material nature, which pervert the genuine emotion and sentiment originally connected with the Lord in the spiritual world. These emotions are integral parts of the soul but without any enmity. These expressions exist to entice the love. In the spiritual world, everything revolves around the involvement in and anticipation of God's love. It involves the association of others who are also experiencing God's love along with the onward reciprocation between the Divine Couple and between the servants of the Lord.

Basically, all activities in the material world are perverted reflections of the activities in the spiritual world. The reflection reminds us of the genuine reality in the spiritual world. We have the duty to reject the illusion and embrace the reality because God Himself exhibits anger. Different pastimes distinctly show Krishna's expression of anger. He excites the devotees by descending and revealing His extraordinary loving affairs along with His warlike activities. He also descends to annihilate the miscreants and the illusions. Sometimes He performs these pastimes out of His expression of transcendental anger.

The Nectar of Instruction, Text 1, describes how to dovetail our anger in devotional service:

> Krishna is just like the sun, and *maya* is
> just like darkness. If the sun is present,
> there is no question of darkness.

Similarly, if Krishna is present in the mind, there is no possibility of the mind's being agitated by *maya's* influence. The yogic process of negating all material thoughts will not help. To try to create a vacuum in the mind is artificial. The vacuum will not remain. However, if one always thinks of Krishna and how to serve Krishna best, one's mind will naturally be controlled. Similarly, anger can be controlled. We cannot stop anger altogether, but if we simply become angry with those who blaspheme the Lord or the devotees of the Lord, we control our anger in Krishna consciousness.[10]

We cannot fully check any of these perverted reflections nor do we want to completely stop them; rather, we want to transcendently repose them in Krishna. We do not want to engage in any of these unhealthy emotions based on unhealthy attachments to materialism. However, by using these emotions to enhance the love and rejuvenate our original consciousness, we will move back very quickly to our original nature.

Developing Genuine Love and Selflessness

We have to deal with mundane anger in our own lives. After reading this section, some of you who felt that you did not have an issue with anger may now realize that you do have this problem in your life. You may need to work more closely on transforming lust into love in order to free yourself from the false ego, which identifies or takes away from the real sense of ego. Accessing more genuine love will help free you from the modes of passion and ignorance that accelerate all of these enemies of the mind.

Most importantly, we should try to broaden our vision by trying to see situations from other people's perspectives. As *sadhus* who want to involve ourselves in the pure, eternal community, we need to develop the mood of Vrndavana or the spiritual world. We cannot become residents of this spiritual community until we develop this mood of selflessness. It is a genuine, intense selflessness that is not just a matter of imposition or artificiality. We do not want to end up practicing to be eternal *karmis* or slaves of our passions. If we hold on too tightly to the duality and secondary considerations, it will take away from our real identity as divine, loving agents of the Supreme Godhead.

Questions and Answers

Question: Sometimes a spiritualist may be very strict in the execution of their spiritual practices but still act very harshly towards the rest of the world. In spite of all their devotional rituals and prayers, they still seem to harbor anger within their hearts. How can one on the spiritual path maintain anger since it directly opposes the purpose and goal of pursuing love of God? And how does a person in this predicament find relief from such negative emotions?

Answer: There are many people embarking on the spiritual journey who very nicely engage in all the rituals and external trappings of the religion but who lack sufficient knowledge. Most importantly, such people often lack deep realizations. When someone serves mechanically, it might look like the genuine activity but it is not. The more that one engages in authentic spiritual practices with knowledge, the more one will benefit from the activity. As a matter of fact, the proper activity performed with proper knowledge will give us a greater chance to receive the benefits. However, if a person wants to receive the highest benefits from proper activities, he or she must even go beyond the platform of *jnana* or knowledge and must connect with *vijnana* or realization. Proper spiritual activities are based on behavior, which involves the **hands**; intellectual understanding that involves the **head**; and deep emotional, loving realizations that involve the **heart**. Many spiritual practices will involve the hands and some will involve the head but few involve the heart.

When a person undergoes austerities, he or she will normally gain strength and power, but if the heart is not opening, such strength and power will be misunderstood and also abused. If the person does not develop deeper realizations, it is only a matter of time before this misuse of power occurs. This explains how a neophyte spiritualist can very nicely engage in executing spiritual practices but still act very harshly. The mechanical activity as well as the possession of knowledge will surely help, but such activities will not fully transform one's personality.

Austerities, sacrifices, and penance fall into the different modes of material nature, which the *Bhagavad-gita* describes as the mode of ignorance, the mode of passion, and the mode of goodness. Religious practices under the mode of ignorance will actually degrade the individual as well as the environment. Religious activities in the mode of passion can be very insensitive to the needs and well-being of other people, and religious activities performed in the mode of goodness will benefit everyone but will still fail to connect very profoundly with the heart which is the door to the soul. Transcendental activities actually function as the key to open up the door of the heart so that one can nourish the soul.

When the spiritualist, who has acquired all kinds of credits from previous spiritual activities, becomes excessively angry, such a person will lose some of these spiritual credits. One of the greatest dangers at this point for the practicing spiritualist involves the false ego and such a person must remain constantly vigilant to keep the false ego in check. In this way, he or she will progress nicely in using their hands, head, and heart uniformly and consistently in the service of the Supreme Lord for the genuine benefit of humanity. Such a person who is conscious of his or her behavior and intellectual understanding and who is constantly opening up the heart will easily finds ways to relieve him or herself from the predicament of negative emotions.

Question: You described a lack of forgiveness as one of the symptoms of anger. When someone hurts us, it can lead to feelings of anger and an inability to forgive. How do we abandon this anger and access forgiveness even if the person continues to seemingly attack or hurt us? Forgiveness seems easier to apply if the other person changes their behavior and possibly even acknowledges their hurtful behavior. However, such a change may not happen immediately so how do we relinquish anger and forgive a person who may even continue to repeatedly hurt us in the present without feelings of remorse?

Answer: Forgiveness does not mean that we turn ourselves into a punching bag so that others can continuously throw blows at us, nor does it mean that we become a doormat for others to walk over and wipe their feet. People should certainly remove themselves from a position in which they function as the target of another's attacks.

Forgiveness does **not** mean the following:

- We feel that the person or people who hurt us should be allowed to continue.

- We feel that what they have done was not really so bad after all.

- We suggest that we were actually wrong instead of the other person.

- We have forgotten the wrong.

- We are totally free of the pain.

- We are ready to act as if nothing has happened.

- We are ready to associate fully with the person.

Forgiveness **does** mean the following:

- We are not going to allow the person who hurt us to continue hurting us by constantly holding onto them or their actions. The more we hold onto the anger associated with the event, the more we allow the person to repeatedly assault us.

- We no longer want to keep living in the past.

- We are ready to live in the present by making healthy choices that are not clouded by past negative influences.

- We are ready to be loving always, not only when someone else acts favorably.

In other words, forgiveness is something we mainly do for ourselves so that we can personally free ourselves from various stagnations because such stagnations can affect us physically, psychologically as well as spiritually. If another person chooses to be continuously obnoxious, we do not want to allow their nonsense to impose itself upon us in any way. We want to be fully free to act in the spirit of love in spite of the environment or the person's actions. The spirit of love entails knowing what is actually best for us as well as knowing what is best for the other person's spiritual well-being. When we hold unhealthy anger, it normally means that we want to retaliate or we want to see the person hurt. Consequently, we must ask ourselves, "How much harm or pain must the person experience before we can release them from our psyche?" Their feelings of remorse or lack of remorse should not really dictate or impose upon our own life.

Question: The scriptures praise such qualities as compassion, forgiveness, peacefulness, and detachment. While an aspiring devotee of God endeavors to acquire these positive qualities, how does he or she simultaneously deal with anger? Since the scriptures define anger as a product of the mode of passion, the devotee may endeavor to repress any anger since it does not indicate a sign of advancement in spiritual life. He or she may even feel guilty if they accidentally exhibit the emotion. However, unless a person acknowledges the anger, it does not seem possible for him or her to overcome the problem. Considering these factors, how do spiritualists acknowledge and express anger in a healthy way that will allow them to move through the problem without abandoning the ideals of the scriptures?

Answer: In certain cases, as we already acknowledged, anger can function in a healthy way. For instance, anger can help protect one in the case of a physical attack or when boundaries are being violated. It can function as a signal to look for deeper issues and as a natural part of the grieving process. It can also help us act when there is blasphemy of God or out of affection and concern for others. This type of anger is necessary, but nevertheless, it should not become excessive. Excessive or negative anger always has a victim, either ourselves or someone else. Anger held within can produce hypertension, ulcers, heart attacks, and a whole host of physical complications. Psychologically, the repressed anger can lead to depression and even neurosis. Of course, we understand the many other sociological and spiritual problems associated with unhealthy anger, either manifest or repressed. It is definitely important to look closer to see if our anger is healthy or unhealthy and if it is being released properly for the benefit of all.

The word "compassion" is the real key. If we think and act out of compassion, we will not be easily angered, and when we do express anger, it will manifest in a healthy way. Furthermore, feeling guilt is not necessarily bad. When we have under or overreacted, we should feel some guilt. The guilt should function as a catalyst to help us act more carefully next time so that we can do the right thing in the right way. The guilt should simply allow us to revisit the activity only long enough to learn the lesson made available for us. However, if it turns into excessive or unhealthy guilt, it will cloud our entire consciousness and will cause us to miss the opportunity to learn, grow, and share in healthy ways.

Question: Why do I become angry when I see shortcomings in myself or in other people? It seems that when I see such weaknesses such as anger, pride, insensitivity, enviousness, insecurity, and so on, it requires more love and compassion rather than anger.

Answer: Sometimes we become angry when we see the shortcomings in others because we lack tolerance and also because they mimic our own faults. However, we should see the shortcomings in others as a mirror to look closer at ourselves. First of all, we can look closer at their particular problem so that we can better understand how to remove it from our own lives if we do in fact have the shortcoming. It will also help us better understand the other person's pain and needs. When we see our own shortcomings, we must have a plan of action so that we can improve our own character.

Try some of the techniques that we have offered previously in the discussion. Try journaling; remind yourself about the physical, psychological, social, and spiritual effects of unhealthy anger; pursue some stress reduction techniques; look to see if you have the trigger thoughts such as the "shoulds" and "blamers"; analyze your anger; see how you can change your "shoulds" and "blamers" to more thoughtful activity; be particularly careful to avoid that which will escalate your anger; and take a closer notice to see if you use your anger as a defense mechanism. Most importantly, take a closer notice of your internal dialogues. When you do this type of processing within yourself, act compassionately by trying to help others who are dealing with anger and also by sharing with them and teaching them ways to better manage their own anger. You should always remind yourself, beloved, that true compassion manifests in positive, productive actions. Therefore, be compassionate towards yourself and be authentically compassionate to others. When you see such shortcomings in yourself as well as in others, let this act as a wakeup call for you to call forth the antidote of compassion. This is the shield of the spiritual warrior.

Chapter 4

Healthy Grieving

na yavad etan mana atma-lingam
samsara-tapavapanam janasya
yac choka-mohamaya-raga-lobha-
vairanubandham mamatam vidhatte

The soul's designation, the mind, is the
cause of all tribulations in the material
world. As long as this fact is unknown
to the conditioned living entity, he has
to accept the miserable condition of the
material body and wander within this
universe in different positions. Because
the mind is affected by disease,
lamentation, illusion, attachment,
greed and enmity, it creates bondage
and a false sense of intimacy within
this material world.
Srimad-Bhagavatam 5.11.16

Healthy Grieving

We want to examine the topic of grief or lamentation as a way to work on ourselves and also to help other people through periods of crisis. As we become more sensitive to some of these issues, we will be able to offer more solace to others. Understanding grief will also assist us in the development of healthy families and communities, and will increase our ability to ward off some of the negativity currently bombarding the planet.

Spiritualists often fall into deeper states of grieving than the materialists, which may sound very strange. Why should people who have a higher understanding about life often grieve more than the materialists or atheists? This occurs because spiritualists often categorize grief as improper or bad, which only compounds the situation when they do fall into a state of grief or pain. Consequently, not only do they lament over a trauma or loss, but they also feel anxiety due to their low state of consciousness. In some cases, a person may fail to actively follow their vows and commitments which make up their identity; therefore, they not only grieve over the tragedy, but they also lament due to their low standard of consciousness and behavior. Spiritualists may have more anxiety because they have the knowledge but cannot seem to act upon what they know.

For example, a very knowledgeable lawyer might know all the rules and have mastered all the techniques of presentation but somehow he still loses the case. This lawyer will undergo more intense grief than a novice who loses because, in spite of all his knowledge and endeavors, he simply could not produce the results. The novice might lose the case due to his own mistake or lack of knowledge; therefore, he will try to learn from the error in order to avoid the same situation in the future. His grief will not be as intense as the expert lawyer who had all the knowledge and skill within him but simply could not transmit it in a sufficient way. Similarly, spiritualists often go through deeper levels of depression due to the complexity of the situation in the material world. Practicing spiritual life in the material arena deals with many contradictions; therefore, people need a more thorough understanding of the events in their own lives as well as within their own families and communities.

In order to thoroughly examine this issue, we will break down the topic into five different sections. First, we want to look deeper into the causes of grief. Secondly, we will examine the various stages that individuals pass through as they grieve. Thirdly, we want to look at the symptoms associated with lamentation. Next, we will try to understand why some people try to avoid or hide from grief. Finally, we want to find ways to positively deal with the issue, which may require different approaches, mindsets, or therapies.

Causes of Grief

Due to the accessibility of information in recent years, people might have more reasons to grieve, especially as they hear about all the catastrophes and disasters occurring all over the world. Each person and family can instantly bring all of these problems into their own homes in a matter of seconds via the television, radio, computer, etc. The increasing illusions also intensify the grief. Since modernity and commercialization throw so much propaganda at people, they have trouble trying to deal with the hard realities when the illusions fall apart. When people cannot substantiate these illusions, they have trouble trying to cope. People also lament due to the shifting job market. There is so much insecurity in the job force, even among people who have degrees and a sense of loyalty to their profession. They will feel intense anxiety and sadness when their seemingly secure jobs suddenly disintegrate. Divorce and especially death obviously lead to grief. Another type of grief can manifest when one makes a strong commitment to follow a spiritual path. One may consciously or even unconsciously grieve about the loss of previous associations and connections.

In one sense, any type of grief is an expression of death since it deals with loss, bewilderment, and disappointment. It could manifest as the physical death of a friend or as the death or loss of a job. Divorce or another type of fragmentation can lead to the death of a relationship. We may also have to accept the death of a particular idea that can no longer provide comfort or security. People even grieve due to the loss of their youth and beauty. They lament as their intelligence slowly diminishes. All of these changes bring about an amazing amount of sadness and depression. Of course, perpetual grief can crystallize into an intense mood of extreme or chronic depression.

The scriptures also describe the unlimited causes of misery and lamentation. The purport of the *Srimad-Bhagavatam* 3.28.32 describes how the miseries in the material world lead to intense lamentation.

> The entire universe is full of miseries, and therefore the inhabitants of this material universe are always shedding tears out of intense grief. There is a great ocean of water made from such tears, but for one who surrenders unto the Supreme Personality of Godhead,

the ocean of tears is at once dried up.
One need only see the charming smile
of the Supreme Lord. In other words,
the bereavement of material existence
immediately subsides when one sees
the charming smile of the Lord.

In spite of the miseries and disappointments that lead to
fear and grief, if we can somehow take shelter of the wonderful
love and beauty of the Lord, then the dualities of the material
world will not influence us to the same extent.

In the second chapter of the *Bhagavad-gita*, Arjuna falls
into an overwhelming state of bewilderment that literally
brings him to tears. The fratricidal war that he must fight is the
source of his lamentation. While Krishna drives his chariot on
the battlefield of Kuruksetra, Arjuna sees great devotees such as
grandfather Bhismadeva and Dronacarya, his worshipful elders
and teachers. He must confront this tremendous challenge,
which involves fighting his exalted superiors due to his duty
as a *ksatriya* or warrior. Arjuna does not see how any action
will lead to a positive outcome. If he defeats his own family
members through war and destruction, he will not find any
happiness. On the other hand, if he just leaves the war and begs
for his livelihood, it will only result in infamy. He would rather
relinquish the benefits of the heavenly kingdoms and material
wealth than live with the anxiety and loss that come from warfare. Therefore, Arjuna says in the *Bhagavad-gita* 2.8:

na hi prapasyami mamapanudyad
yac chokam ucchosanam indriyanam
avapya bhumav asapatnam rddham
rajyam suranam api cadhipatyam

> I can find no means to drive away this
> grief which is drying up my senses. I
> will not be able to dispel it even if I
> win a prosperous, unrivaled kingdom
> on earth with sovereignty like the
> demigods in heaven.

Due to his overwhelming grief, Arjuna searches for a way out. In his state of bewilderment, he cannot understand how a war against his own family members can be ethical or moral. The entire *Bhagavad-gita* begins with this dilemma. Arjuna sees a "no win" situation and he cannot decide how to act. Several verses later, the Lord tells Arjuna:

> *asocyan anvasocas tvam*
> *prajna-vadams ca bhasase*
> *gatasun agatasums ca*
> *nanusocanti panditah*

> While speaking learned words, you
> are mourning for what is not worthy
> of grief. Those who are wise lament
> neither for the living nor for the dead.
> *Bhagavad-gita* 2.11

Even in the presence of real intelligence and spiritual understanding, a person is still confronted with many dilemmas. Issues will always confront us but they do not disturb a wise person. In this verse, Krishna is basically asking Arjuna, "Are you really intelligent?" Arjuna seems to be speaking eloquent and profound words like a wise man, but the meaning of his words does not indicate actual wisdom. Since his type of lamentation falls into the category of ignorance, Krishna helps him reflect more on real knowledge. The Lord explains that one who has a higher understanding does not lament because such knowledge will help one understand why certain events unfold in a person's life and how to act accordingly. The purport to *Srimad-Bhagavatam* 4.26.1-3 discusses another cause of lamentation:

> The living entity sits in one place only. The causes of his bondage are two: namely lamentation and illusion. In material existence the living entity simply hankers to get something he can never get. Therefore he is in illusion. As a result of being in this illusory situation, the living entity is always lamenting. Thus lamentation and illusion are described herein as dvikubara, the two posts of bondage.

Stages of Grief

The Roller Coaster

In our second category, we want to examine the stages that people move through as they deal with grief. We can actually compare the process of lamentation to a roller coaster ride. While riding on a roller coaster, a person naturally expects some shock, bewilderment, adventure, and even fear. Sometimes people even get on that ride in order to experience the adrenalin rush and the adventure. However, if they realize what the ride entails, they will be able to bear some of the challenges without jumping overboard when the roller coaster speeds up.

Every day, I receive letters and e-mails mainly from spiritualists and students all over the world whose challenges often deal with loss and bereavement in different ways. Obviously, we must all confront grief directly due to the deaths of our countrymen, friends, and family. I realize that some people are having or will have great difficulties moving through the stages of grieving. When some people experience a serious loss, they never move out of the shock stage. Other people will remain in denial about a tragedy that happened fifteen or even thirty years ago. These people will carry dysfunctional patterns in their consciousness and in their socialization due to the stagnation. For this reason, we want to share these points as a way to assist many people and to help them look first at themselves. We have all had so many seemingly unfortunate situations to grieve about, and in some cases, we have not properly resolved the issues. These patterns may even create distractions in our spiritual lives because we have not come to sufficient resolutions. We also want to help other people through their times of need because people need the most help and support during the grieving process. We must all inevitably face these periods of lamentation and grief.

Understanding the Eight Stages of Grief

1. **Shock** is one of the first stages in the grieving process. It deals more with the physicality, which also relates to the subtle or psychological aspect. Shock often acts as a support, which helps the person deal with the immediate anxiety, fear, and loss. It practically numbs a person. For instance, if someone has a serious car accident, the pain may intensify to such a degree that the body just falls unconscious. The body has a natural way of dealing with the tremendous impact of an accident.

2. After shock comes **denial** in which a person tries to deny the reality. They might even convince themselves that the tragedy did not occur. If a person's beloved died, he or she might continue to act as if the beloved still lives. For instance, a widow might continue to cook for two or arrange the table according to her past habits. In this way, a person can avoid a difficult reality that might simply overwhelm him or her.

3. Then we will see a progression towards the next stage, which involves **anger**. A person will begin to think, "How could my beloved leave me in this position? How could he mistreat me in such a horrible way? How could she sack me?" For many people, this anger stays for their entire lifetime. In some cases, it even travels on into other lifetimes because the most prominent issues in our consciousness will follow us into future lives. Sometimes we have brought them in from a previous life just as we bring forth patterns from our childhood. For example, the traumas, which result from child abuse in the early part of a person's life, will affect the person unless he or she deals with the issue in a proper way. Anger sets in when a person feels that another individual has put them into this state of bereavement and loss.

4. At this point, people may begin to feel **guilt**. They internalize the anger and it begins to eat at them. They feel guilty that they did not prevent the incident, and in some cases, they feel it should have happened to themselves rather than to the other person.

5. **Fear** is the next stage. A person may fear that the tragedy

will happen again or it will happen to oneself. For example, if a mother loses a child, either in pregnancy or in another type of situation, she will develop so much fear about the possibility of losing another child again in the future. She may then overcompensate by trying to protect the next child out of fear of another loss. The mother may even avoid chastising or correcting the child, and this will cause her to nurture the child in an unhealthy way due to the previous disappointment.

6. The sixth stage involves **pain** and **sorrow**. Of course, fear and pain somewhat permeate all of these stages in various ways; however, it becomes more prominent at this point. The pain exists in the shock stages but it remains in the background due to the numbness. In the period of denial, the person represses the pain and sadness. It is dangerous because if a person continues to repress instead of genuinely grieving, he or she will not be able to move to the next step or grow from the experience.

7. The seventh stage involves the **acceptance** of the reality along with a resolution or conclusion. Not only should the spiritualist find a resolution, but he or she should also acquire realization, compassion, and a greater sense of empathy. If a person moves through these stages in a healthy way, it can conclude with tremendous realizations and growth.

8. The final stage involves **returning to pursuits of love**. The grieving person has moved through the healing process and is progressive. He remembers the love for the person whose association he no longer has and now

allows that love to come forth. This replaces shock, denial, anger, guilt, pain, and sorrow. At this point, the individual experiences empathy, compassion, and powerful realizations.

After reflecting on these issues more closely, I realized that some devotees who have lost their *guru* or spiritual mentor get stuck in some of these stages. Some of them will remain in denial or shock for a period of time and others will just feel angry. They will ask, "How could my *guru* leave me. How did the institution or God allow this to happen?" They might even feel angry with themselves for not preventing the tragedy. People begin to feel responsible or they may hold anger at their spiritual mentor and even at God Himself. Many people do not move beyond these points and many of us in our own communities will also have problems moving through these stages. Consequently, they will carry these emotions into their relationships with their spouse, children, associates, or God.

Developing Empathy

People cannot always reach deeper levels in their own psyche or understand another person's psyche unless they have gone through some trauma, pain, or grief themselves. It is through these experiences that a person gains enrichment if they come out of it successfully. In many cases, **the only way to deal with pain is to go through the pain**. We have to recognize it and identify it within ourselves. We need to **name it, face it, feel it, and release it**. As we deal with anger and conflict resolution as well, we must bring forth the issue and identify it before we can rectify the problem. If we do not identify the issue, it might just fall into the background and manifest at other times. We must face it in order to release it. It is healthy to move through these stages and come out on the other side as an enriched person who has deeper realizations and deeper levels of compassion. A successful person will have a greater ability to help others who may get stuck at different levels.

Symptoms of Grief

People exhibit a variety of emotions and behaviors when they fall into states of grief. They may feel extreme despair, anger, or sadness and physically, they may feel exhausted, depleted, and anti-social. There is no limit to the way in which people react to grief. It will affect each person in a different way. Grief creates a feeling of distance from God. Many times when we grieve, we feel that God gave us a bad deal. We wonder why Krishna allowed such a painful situation to manifest in our lives. We ask, "Why me instead of the millions of other people in the world? Why did my child or my spouse have to die? Why did I lose my job instead of someone else?" We may question God since He ultimately controls everything. We may wonder how a merciful and kind God could allow such a horrible or evil thing to happen. Unfortunately, some people will simply resort to atheism. On the other hand, a calamity or trauma might act as a catalyst to bring a person closer to God and help them think more about their spiritual alignments. However, seemingly negative situations generally cause a person to question God's justice.

Hopelessness is another symptom of grief. We all have brief periods of disappointment and hopelessness, but for some people, this hopelessness will not dissipate; rather, it just festers year after year. They will even lose any desire for social exchange. Furthermore, the symptoms of grief make it more

difficult to progress because the behavior
diametrically opposes the behavior that help
ticular problem. For instance, if someone d
benevolence, a person can take it to the Lord in order to find
a positive resolution. However, a person in a state of intense
grief will often do just the opposite and prolong the situation.
A person who feels anti-social may actually need good association to transcend the misery. It might actually help the person to
associate with people who will support them and allow them to
cry and share. These other people can call the griever out of his
or her sadness. However, the person often wants to back away
from socialization.

Grief also drains our enthusiasm and passion. In this case,
we may actually need some project or goal to carry us to the
next step. However, we usually avoid that which will help the
most and we continue to grieve. A person in this state will
also feel physically and emotionally empty and drained. Grief
can lead to a state of self-pity and even fear. The griever may
simply remain in the past and fear the future. However, he or
she needs to accept and honor the future in order to move on.
Feelings of anger and loneliness often manifest as well. The
person may even neglect proper hygiene, suffer from insomnia,
and lose their appetite.

Once I observed my own reaction to a foolish and dis-
appointing mistake my secretary made. While trying to fax
a plane ticket to a travel agent, the fax machine just ripped
the ticket apart. Initially, I felt anger due to the complication
involving Krishna's money along with the time that we would
spend dealing with the problem. I wondered why my secretary
could not perform such a simple task properly and pay more
attention to his service. While reflecting on this situation later,
I realized that the anger resulted from grief and actually pro-

vided a way to deal with the grief. I felt sadness while watching this five hundred dollar plane ticket to England just disappear since it would now require additional arrangements. However, if I had faxed the ticket myself, I would have immediately felt sadness rather than anger, but since my secretary faxed the ticket, I reacted with anger. If I had ripped the ticket, I would personally have had to take responsibility. Later, I would have even thought of the different ways that I could have avoided the mistake. We will process situations differently according to the various factors involved. If something happens to our own community, spouse, children, or even ourselves, we will process a situation in a unique way. As we look deeper into this issue of grief, we will also have to move out of our own comfort zone in order to consider the needs of others. We want to find the best way to bring solace and an actual solution.

Why People Avoid Grief

When people do not have a certain amount of healthy grieving, it can lead to sicknesses and mental disturbances. It can create so many unhealthy personality problems. If a person does not deal with the grief in a healthy way, it will continue to attack him or her again and again. It will not simply go away. Sometimes it will surface when a person least expects it and he or she will find it harder to deal with at such times. It is better for a person to **name it, face it, feel it, and release it** in order to genuinely let go and grow from the experience.

Some people claim that they do not want to wallow in misery because it does not seem proper. Some cultures even look down upon men who cry or show too much emotion. Grieving often relates to the cultural norms because people grieve according to their hereditary and environmental concerns. In such cases, people might want to appear strong. Some people may even be afraid to show emotion. In other instances, a person may feel that if they forget the tragedy and go into denial, the pain will just go away. Furthermore, we may not want to draw attention to ourselves. Some people feel that if they openly grieve within the community, they will draw too much attention to themselves instead of to the person or the *guru* who has left. We can see the danger because they will miss the opportunity to shed the pain and grow by sharing within the community.

People's lifestyles also prevent time for healthy grieving. If they have full time jobs along with a family, they may simply become absorbed with their work and their children. When they come home from work, the six o'clock news overwhelms them with other tragedies and they just cannot actually take the necessary time. For their own survival, some people simply cannot process the grief because it comes at them from so many different sectors. Since they want to maintain some sense of stability and equilibrium, they think that they can avoid it by not addressing the deeper issues. Some people recognize that pride prevents them from acknowledging the hurt because they cannot humble themselves. They do not want other people to see the sadness because they fear that others will label it as a weakness.

Some people genuinely do not have enough deep compassion or interest in others to grieve for them. In some cases, people just do not care or cannot sympathize due to their superficiality. Consequently, the seemingly painful situation simply does not affect their psyche. They do not have this feeling of *param-duhkha-duhkhi-krpam-buddhi* in which one feels the pain and sadness of another person as well as their happiness. They really do not feel connected with anybody, which means that they do not have any real reason to grieve. Either they do not feel connected to the issue or they never allow themselves to experience that pain. Such people will have all types of problems and even sicknesses because the emotion has to go somewhere. Devotees especially may not consider lamentation to be a part of spiritual life. Even in the *Bhagavad-gita*, Krishna tells Arjuna that the wise lament neither for the living or the dead. Sometimes devotees avoid grief because they want to act on the highest platform of God consciousness. Devotees sometimes think that one in Krishna consciousness should not grieve because the scriptures declare that we are not these bodies. The scriptures instruct us to remain detached and grief seems to indicate attachment; therefore, a person may prefer to suffer peacefully and deny the issue even though it later surfaces in unhealthy ways. Sometimes the denial, shock, and anger overwhelm us to such an extent that refusal becomes part of the denial. The mind might rationalize or minimize the situation but then we just repress it due to our confusion. Later it will come out in our behaviors and personalities.

From some of the statements in the scriptures, it may in fact seem unhealthy to lament:

sanjaya uvaca
tam tatha krpayavistam
asru-purnakuleksanam
visidantam idam vakyam
uvaca madhusudanah

Sanyaja said: Seeing Arjuna full of compassion, his mind depressed, his eyes full of tears, Madhusudana,

Krishna, spoke the following words.
Bhagavad-gita 2.1

Srila Prabhupada writes in his purport:

> Material compassion, lamentation and tears are all signs of ignorance of the real self. Compassion for the eternal soul is self-realization. The word 'Madhusudana' is significant in this verse. Lord Krishna killed the demon Madhu, and now Arjuna wanted Krishna to kill the demon of misunderstanding that had overtaken him in the discharge of his duty. No one knows where compassion should be applied. Compassion for the dress of a drowning man is senseless. A man fallen in the ocean of nescience cannot be saved simply by rescuing his outward dress—the gross material body. One who does not know this and laments for the outward dress is called a sudra, or one who laments unnecessarily.
> *Bhagavad-gita* 2.1, purport

When devotees hear this verse, they may think that all lamentation means the acceptance of the bodily platform of life. However, the verse does not suggest that we should categorize all types of grief as forms of *maya* or illusion.

Techniques to Deal with Grief

Look for the Solution

We will now offer several techniques to help us deal with grief in a healthy manner. We want to act positively so that the grief will end with greater realizations, empathy, and compassion. In this way, we will emerge from the crisis as empowered spiritual warriors ready to assist others, especially those who get stuck at particular levels.

The *Srimad-Bhagavatam* 4.8.24 explains that one should find a solution and use his or her energy to resolve the problem instead of wallowing in grief.

> *maitreya uvaca*
> *evam sanjalpitam matur*
> *akarnyarthagamam vacah*
> *sanniyamyatmanatmanam*
> *niscakrama pituh purat*

The great sage Maitreya continued: The instruction of Dhruva Maharaja's mother, Suniti, was actually meant for fulfilling his desired objective. Therefore, after deliberate consideration and with intelligence and fixed determination, he left his father's house.

Srila Prabhupada writes in the purport:

Both the mother and the son were lamenting Dhruva Maharaja's having

been insulted by his stepmother
his father's not having taken any
on this issue. But mere lament:
is useless—one should find out the
means to mitigate one's lamentation.
Thus both mother and son decided to
take shelter of the lotus feet of the Lord
because that is the only solution to all
material problems.

Techniques for Application

1. **Writing or journaling** can help a person in a state of grief
   who has lost someone dear to him or her. They can write
   a letter to their beloved in order to communicate their
   feelings or even talk to the individual as a way to bring
   healthy closure.

2. Some of the same **relievers of stress** will also help a person deal with grief such as exercise, meditation, diet, and
   so on. Affirmations and visualizations will help harness
   the mind and help us change our behavior and understanding. Massages will sometimes help to relieve some
   of the stress and tension in the physical body that also
   affects the mind. When a person does not grieve, it must
   go somewhere. Some experts say that it goes particularly
   into the heart and arms just as anxiety affects certain
   organs and different aspects of the body.

3. We should recognize the importance of **sharing within
   the community**. In Ethiopia, some communities have an
   interesting ritual to deal with grief or loss. If a mother
   loses her child, the community gathers the mother's

closest friends and relatives, and as a group, they go to the mother's house. Then the person closest to the mother will act as the main spokesperson and give her the message. When they give the message, they then collectively go through the most intense part of the grieving together at that moment. They will all cry, embrace, and share together so that the person can release much of the pain immediately. Consequently, the mother will have less baggage to deal with at a later time. In this way, she knows that she has a support system that she can always connect with in times of pain. If compassionate and loving people communicate the news, the griever will feel this care and love so that the transmission will not create even more anxiety, loneliness, anger, or frustration.

Usually, we just call the person in an impersonal way because we simply do not know how to act. We may even avoid a person in grief for the same reasons. Instead of allowing them to cry and share their pain, which will also involve us, we often just avoid them. However, if the community supports the individual by sharing the bad news as a unit, it will come through a level of communication that gives love and care to the actual person. Then the person will not feel intimidated to express his or her own grief. It sends a message to the person that we understand their pain and we will experience it with them because we love and care for them. We all want to grow from the trauma and come out stronger in our relationships.

The Native Americans have a slogan, "After a night of grief, what will you do to save the children?" It basically indicates that we should honor the grief and the reality, but we should then use that to create better families and communities. What will we do with that to create growth for the future? How will we set up an arrangement and an environment that will make it easier for others to handle the same issue? How will we all grow though this like a tragic hero who comes out of the situation with more profound realizations? How will we come out of this as greater spiritual warriors?

4. **Fear, anger, and grief do not exist**. What do we mean by this statement? Do they have a certain weight, color, or appearance? Can you draw them, see them, or talk to them? They do not really exist. Their existence depends only on a perception that we create according to past circumstances. We often embrace certain mindsets such as grief according to external situations although the grief entity itself has no connection to these events. There is no such thing as a grief entity. It simply depends on our codification of a situation. This means that grief, anger and depression need a host. They need someone to invite them in and nourish them. We can deal with grief as we would deal with any temporary visitor. We allow them to stay for a few days but they must eventually leave our home. We have the right to invite them permanently into our house or we have the ability to honor their existence while still encouraging them to continue on their journey. We create grief according to how we codify certain situations. According to that codification, we turn grief into an entity of its own.

5. **All suffering has a deeper hidden meaning that we can uncover.** We can either view the world as an abode of suffering which leads us to cynicism and depression or we can understand that God allows suffering as a way to

educate the living entities on their misbehavior. Instead of just seeing God as a tyrant, autocrat, or as unmerciful, we can accept the grief to be a part of the reality of the material world. These experiences are natural and sometimes even healthy if we learn and grow from them.

6. **Ultimately, when we gain real knowledge, we will not experience ongoing lamentation.** A person in knowledge will feel joy and security since they know that Krishna will ultimately take care of them. However, it does not mean that we should not face certain problems and move through them so that they can help us grow and advance. In the following lecture given by Srila Prabhupada on the *Srimad-Bhagavatam* 6.1.15, he helps us understand that we will feel joyful and abandon grief after we gain real knowledge:

> Krishna says in the *Bhagavad-gita*: *brahma-bhutah prasannatma (Bg. 18.54)*. As soon as you get right knowledge, you become jolly. First jolliness is due to 'Oh, I was in such false notion so long. Oh, how fool I was.' Then you become happy that 'Now I am no longer fool. I was thinking that I'm God. But now I can understand that I am God's eternal servant.' That gives him liberation and he becomes *prasannatma*, jolly. Because that is the right situation. *Brahma-bhutah prasannatma, na socati nakanksati (Bg. 18.54). Na*

socati. He has no lamentation. Because if anyone knows that I am a small particle, spiritual spark, and protected by the Supreme Lord, then where there is scope of my lamentation? Just like a small child, so long he knows that 'My father is standing by me, I am free. Nobody can touch my body...' Because he's confident that if there is any danger, 'My father is there.' Similarly, this surrender means completely to have to have faith that 'I have no danger because God, Krishna, is protecting me. I am now fully surrendered, *prasannatma.*'[11]

Focusing on Growth and Healing

When we lose someone very dear to us, we can actually honor them best by moving through the healthy grieving process since it will help us reflect on their meaning in our lives. However, we can honor them in the best way by transcending the grief because it allows the love connected with the other person to live through us by constantly feeling gratitude for whatever good knowledge, good association, and good feelings they gave us. However, if we kill ourselves emotionally through repression or denial, we will minimize their gifts and we will overlook the value and worth that their existence should continually have in our lives. If we get stuck in any of the stages of grief, we will not honor our beloved sufficiently due to anger, guilt, shock, or denial.

By growing from the experience, we will allow that love and association to live on with us and through us. When Srila Prabhupada, one of the great Vaisnava scholars and mentors for myself and thousands of others, left his body, if we simply went into states of anger or denial, we would have minimized his existence and his offering to the world. However, if we accept the situation by becoming more determined, loyal, accountable, and empathetic, we will feel more energized by his offering to us. By honoring him in such a powerful way, he will live through us and we will also wholesomely grow as a result of the experience.

Not only can grief help us honor the existence of another person, but it can also function as a type of purification in our own spiritual growth. In the purport to the song *Gaura Pahu* by Narottama dasa Thakura, Srila Prabhupada says in a lecture on January 10, 1969:

> Those who are too much attached to materialistic way of life, or always drinking the poison of sense gratification, they are not attracted by the *sankirtana* movement. So at the last, Narottama dasa Thakura is lamenting. He's not lamenting. He's representing ourself. If one comes to that point of lamentation, that is also very nice. He immediately becomes purified. Lamentation means purification. So he says, *keno va achaya prana ki sukha paiya...* 'Why I am living? I do not make association with the devotees. I do not take part in the *sankirtana*

movement. I do not understand
is Krishna. I do not understand
is Lord Caitanya. Then what fo
living?' This is lamentation. 'What is
my happiness? What is the standard
of my happiness? Why I am living?'
Narottama dasa keno na gelo. 'Why
I did not die long, long ago? I should
have died. What is the meaning of my
living?' So it is not Narottama dasa
Thakura's lamentation.[12]

We are allowing this process of healing and purification
to become a very integral part of all of the rural communities
I supervise around the world. We plan to add a hospice that
will act as a catalyst for more healing modalities and facilities
to take place. It will hopefully also increase our ability to take
care of the mind, body, and soul together. We want to have more
wonderful facilities for alternative health because spiritual life
should be the real remedy for illnesses along with the illusions.
We want the ability to repair that which has broken in order to
offer it back to God. It does not simply involve well-wishing
but it requires practical strategy. We must genuinely want to
understand someone else's pain and have sufficient communication. Sometimes we cannot help another person because we
only see our own pain or we only see what we want to see. We
may even consider the person to be in *maya* and simply tell
them to get out of their illusion. However, for a person in a state
of intense grief and depression, it is not that easy to transcend
the pain. They need someone to consistently guide them in a
loving but stern way. They mainly need a hospital for the heart
equipped with tolerant, compassionate, understanding, loving
spiritual warriors.

Transcendental Grief

Grief is actually most natural because it really stems from our separation from God. Ultimately, because of our separation from the Supreme Lord and from our original environment and relationships, we have an underlying grief that always remains with us. We are away from that environment which can give us the highest level of satisfaction, fulfillment, realization, and joy. The purport to *Srimad-Bhagavatam* 9.11.16 emphasizes that transcendental grief exists in the spiritual realm in its highest connection with God:

> Lord Ramacandra's grief at the news of Sitadevi's entering the earth is not to be considered material. In the spiritual world also there are feelings of separation, but such feelings are considered spiritual bliss. Grief in separation exists even in the Absolute, but such feelings of separation in the spiritual world are transcendentally blissful. Such feelings are a sign of *tasya prema-vasyatva-svabhava*, being under the influence of *hladini-sakti* and being controlled by love. In the material world such feelings of separation are only a perverted reflection.

In other words, grief also exists in the spiritual world but its perverted material counterpart significantly differs from the original source. Even in the spiritual world, the entities constantly want to engage in more pastimes with Krishna and this constant reflection of separation produces transcendental grief.

Questions and Answers

Question: We understand that some devotees may develop suicidal tendencies due to grief and loss. In the song written by Narottama dasa Thakura, he also expresses his desire to give up his life. How do we distinguish between these two expressions of lamentation or grief?

Answer: As Srila Prabhupada says in the purport, Narottama dasa Thakura does in fact lament but he also shows us what we should do with that despair. Essentially, a person should face the weakness or dilemma with a sense of regret and intensity but then he or she should use that intensity to move out of the stagnation. A person can think, "Why should I live? Why should my life go on with all of my weaknesses?" However, he or she should utilize these feelings to make a positive change. If the person allows that suicidal emotion to stay, he or she will get stuck with guilt and anger. It is unhealthy to avoid the situation or think that it will just somehow disappear on its own. If we do not properly deal with them, these hidden emotions will come to haunt us at later times. It is also unhealthy to recognize these feelings in a way that just feeds their negativity and helps them to grow. It is healthy to recognize the problem and use it to improve on our own qualities.

People who have such intense suicidal reflections have usually turned their anger inward. We can look at depression as anger that people have towards themselves. It deals with disappointments and with some aspect of death, either a physical death or death to some aspiration in their lives such as a job or prestige. However, we need to understand that a failure does not categorize the person as a total failure. If a person has a problem, it does not form his or her entire identity.

Question: When I heard of the passing of one recent spiritual mentor, I think I went through all of those stages. However, at one point, I realized that I did not grieve solely for him but I felt for his disciples as well. After about three days, I accepted my grief but I then focused on my own situation and thought of you, as my spiritual director. What if it had been you?

This morning I realized that if sudden death came upon me, I might not be able to remember Krishna. Then I read on the internet several verses from the eighth chapter of the *Bhagavad-gita* which explain the auspicious times that a *yogi* should leave his or her body. However, a person in full God consciousness does not need to worry about such details because he has attained Krishna consciousness. I do not feel that I have attained a high enough level of Krishna consciousness. However, at 75 years of age, death really can come at the next moment but, after having these realizations, I do not feel ready in my consciousness. I have been reflecting on all of these questions in the last few days and I do not know where I am at after all of these years of spiritual disciplines. However, I feel that I am changing in a way that I cannot even recognize. I want to try to grasp this strength in spite of whatever happens to you or to any of the devotees, but I feel that I have a long way to go. Can you help me with this internal struggle?

Answer: At your point in life, it is natural for you to more realistically look at the transition in a way that goes beyond theory. We see that the Lord has made certain promises. In *Bhagavad-gita* 18.66, Krishna tells us not to worry, hesitate, or fear:

sarva-dharman parityajya
mam ekam saranam vraja
aham tvam sarva-papebhyo
moksayisyami ma sucah

Abandon all varieties of religion and
just surrender unto Me. I shall deliver
you from all sinful reactions. Do not
fear.

Throughout the *Bhagavad-gita*, the Lord gives us so much
knowledge and *dharma* or religion but, at the end, He tells us
to just abandon all varieties of religion. He does not want us to
just superficially abandon religion but He wants us to go deeper
and connect as best as possible with the essence.

The Supreme Lord says in the *Bhagavad-gita* 4.11:

ye yatha mam prapadyante
tams tathaiva bhajamy aham
mama vartmanuvartante
manusyah partha sarvasah

As all surrender unto Me, I reward them
accordingly. Everyone follows My path
in all respects, O son of Prtha.

The Lord emphatically states that He will reciprocate with His
devotees according to their level of surrender. They do not
have to fear or worry. The chapter that you mentioned from
the *Bhagavad-gita*, especially texts 8.23 and 8.24, describe in
detail the appropriate time for a *yogi* to leave his body. For a
yogi, these details are very important, but the time and place are
not necessarily as important for a devotee because Krishna has

made a promise to His devotees. To the extent that we devote ourselves, Krishna, who resides in the heart and gives us access to *sadhu*, *sastra*, and *guru*, will now facilitate us. He mainly assists us through the agency of *guru*.

At the time of death, the relationship between the *guru* and the disciple is of ultimate importance. Due to the disciple's dedication and service, the *guru* now has the position to connect with the disciple and facilitate him or her during the transition. For example, a young businessman might not have so much capital but he tries so hard to succeed in the business world. As a result, a wealthy person may see this young man and decide to help him succeed. The wealthy man acts as a financer or lawyer who helps him and pleads for his case. Similarly, a devotee may not have reached a level of full purity but may still receive the highest result. For instance, in terms of some of the disciples of certain pure teachers, some may not be fully pure but, when they leave the body, they may still go directly back to the spiritual world because of their intense degree of dedication. The spiritual master will reach out and bring such a person back home as a result of the student's seriousness. Out of his mercy, the first class spiritual mentor will aid and compliment that disciple in his or her weak areas. It is as if the spiritual master is supplying additional capital or intervening as a lawyer to help his dedicated disciple who needs just a little facilitation for his life to be fully successful.

In other words, we need to realize the importance of remaining loyal in our daily lives to our connection with the *parampara* or the bona fide chain of pure and potent spiritual mentors. Furthermore, as spiritual masters, we must develop the spiritual potency to execute our necessary services on all levels. However, if the individual devotee follows the instructions of the scriptures, associates with devotees, and follows the instructions of the *guru* with dedication, even if the *guru* does not have the potency or purity to bring the disciple to the spiritual world, Krishna will do it Himself. Krishna's reciprocation can even manifest in the form of the spiritual master who will distinctly reach out and bring that person back. In some cases, the disciple can actually bring the *guru* back to the spiritual world. A disciple may develop such purity that he or she may even return before the *guru* and bring the *guru* back. Krishna will certainly accommodate such a devotee.

Furthermore, this shows the beauty of the relationship between the *guru* and the disciple, which is interwoven in the most dynamic way. We understand that one way in which a person can return to the spiritual world is just through the blessings of a pure devotee. We must not minimize the importance of advancing in the community of devotees. Similarly, we must recognize and search for the advanced souls and sincerely serve them. We understand that even the *prasadam* or food remnants of a pure soul have potency. Narada Muni, a great angelic being, previously made tremendous advancement simply by taking the association of elevated devotees, honoring their remnants and serving them. The Lord has provided so many types of help but, surprisingly, we often lose our courage and run away from the healthiest activities.

We should continue without hesitation or fear because Krishna made these promises Himself and He has the responsibility to do the necessary. For this reason, we must not develop the mentality of a cult by considering the *guru* to be only his body. Such followers will only be able to follow the physical instructions or will feel too emotional about the body. We accept a spiritual mentor because we want to get Krishna and Krishna will facilitate. For this reason, when a devotee's *guru* falls down, we want to encourage them to remain on the spiritual path since the *guru* just acts as the door to the Godhead. The Lord always monitors every situation and He will arrange additional doors to help that person.

Unfortunately, most of the time when a *guru* falls or has trouble, the disciples gradually fall away, weaken, and many times even leave the process. However, it means that they did not really understand the process in the first place. We follow the process as a way to reach Krishna. For instance, in the Bible the Prodigal Son wants to return to the Father and the Father sends another son to assist him in this endeavor. However, the Father remains the facilitator, which means that if His representative deviates, He will certainly make another arrangement to help the son. The Father wants to bring the son back home since he is also ready to return. Similarly, since the disciple may want to come back, the Lord will now facilitate. According to the sincerity of the disciple, Krishna will offer assistance. We just have to remain loyal to our *acaryas* or bona fide teachers and try to give up the anxiety.

The process is powerful but also dangerous. In general, many religions do not place as much emphasis on the relationship between the mentor and the student as in the transcendental process. Due to so many cheaters, many aspiring spiritualists are minimizing the importance of having caring, potent spiritual directors. For this reason, the Supreme Lord arranges to give us scriptures, saints, and teachers. If we sincerely follow the practices that God has given us for our growth and reformation, it will carry us into the spiritual world. In this practice, one embraces love, faithfulness, accountability, loyalty, and selflessness because these qualities are an inherent part of our original identity. As we regain our identity, we can escape from the material prison and fully embrace our eternal, loving state.

Krishna arranged the process and He also evaluates. He

will either allow our spiritual mentor to continue to perfect his duty of bringing us to Him, or if the spiritual master somehow cannot complete his duty and the disciple remains devoted, Krishna Himself has the duty to assist. He will either send help or come Himself in the form of *guru* to bring that disciple back home. In the story of Bali Maharaja in the Vedic scriptures, His *guru* lost focus but Krishna came as Vamanadeva to benedict Bali Maharaja due to his steady dedication. We can just see the awesomeness of devotional service.

In terms of death, we do not really grieve excessively when someone leaves, especially if the person has served with devotion and dedication. We feel happy that the person has gone to the spiritual kingdom and attained such a glorious victory. It should encourage us to perform our own service so that we can join them. We can simultaneously pray that they will help us speed up as we endeavor to also return home and that we can know them in their actual identity in our service to the Godhead.

Question: When we get hurt, we often hide our vulnerability due to false pride, and this prevents us from trusting the Lord and the devotees. However, we must have the faith that He will never give us anything that we cannot handle.

Answer: Krishna will not give us any challenge beyond our ability to handle. It is an illusion to think that we have more than we can bear or that certain experiences in our lives do not come from our *karma*. For this reason, we need the healthy grieving process because it helps us honor God's position as the Supreme Controller. He does not make mistakes; rather, every single event in our lives has a reason and a purpose. It happens to us instead of to someone else for a specific reason as well.

When we look closer, we can always go deeper and try to connect with the Lord rather than run away or become angry with Him. As we recognize that such challenges comprise our experience, we will engage in the nine-fold devotional process or the full process of devotional service with determination. Although these practices are an essential part of our existence, we will not engage in them with profundity if we have too much guilt, anger, fear, denial, or shock in the back of our minds. We want to honor grief while simultaneously endeavoring to rise above it.

Chapter 5

Coping with Depression

sidac cittam viliyeta
cetaso grahane 'ksamam
mano nastam tamo glanis
tamas tad upadharaya

When one's higher awareness fails
and finally disappears and one is thus
unable to concentrate his attention, his
mind is ruined and manifests ignorance
and depression. You should understand
this situation to be the predominance of
the mode of ignorance.
Srimad-Bhagavatam 11.25.18

The Age of Kali

yada mayanrtam tandra
nidra himsa visadanam
soka-mohau bhayam dainyam
sa kalis tamasah smrtah

When there is a predominance of
cheating, lying, sloth, sleepiness,
violence, depression, lamentation,
bewilderment, fear and poverty, that
age is Kali, the age of the mode of
ignorance.

Srimad-Bhagavatam 12.3.30

The Age of Kali or the age of quarrel, confusion, and ignorance is mentioned in many religious texts as a time of great
sin and darkness. Increase in depression is a sign of a rapidly
deteriorating civilization and an extremely frustrated and disappointed citizenry.

Mental Illness on the Rise

After extensive research, the World Health Organization
reported on the condition of mental health around the world in
their 2001 World Health Report. They estimated that 450 million people on the planet have a mental or behavioral disorder.
Furthermore, depression is now a leading cause of disability
around the world, and, among the ten leading causes of the
global burden of disease, it ranks fourth. The World Health
Organization estimates that, in the next twenty years, depres-

sion will move up the list to become the second leading cause of disease. They also report that one million people commit suicide every year and between ten and twenty million make an attempt.[13]

Many elements can contribute to mental illnesses such as biological, psychological, and social factors. Depression can stem from people's increasing dissatisfaction with their husband, wife, children, politicians, religious leaders, educational institutions, themselves, and so on. Even the attachment to materialism will create many problems. All these sources of disappointment lead to stress, anxiety, frustration, and gloom.

By understanding the effects of mental disturbances on the consciousness, we as spiritualists can more effectively assist people who suffer from some of these problems. It is also important for us to know how to help our families and ourselves. The spiritual warrior must protect the healthy and serve the wounded. In order to equip ourselves, we will examine mental illness, and specifically depression, from a biological, psychological, and of course a spiritual perspective.

Who Comes to Devotional Service

Before delving fully into the topic of depression, I would like to offer some background information that can help us understand this issue from a grander perspective. In the *Bhagavad-gita*, Krishna describes the four types of people who come to devotional service:

catur-vidha bhajante mam
janah sukrtino 'rjuna
arto jijnasur artharthi
jnani ca bharatarsabha

> O best among the Bharatas, four kinds
> of pious men begin to render devotional
> service unto Me—the distressed, the
> desirer of wealth, the inquisitive, and
> he who is searching for knowledge of
> the Absolute.
>
> *Bhagavad-gita* 7.16

Only one out of these four types of people actually seeks knowledge of God. The others come to the process of devotional service out of curiosity, distress, or a desire for wealth. The majority of people turn to God when they have issues in their lives which means that they basically approach God because they want Him to remove their material distress and obstacles, enabling them to enjoy or at least suffer more peacefully. However, the most evolved devotees of the Lord are not just interested in orthodoxy; rather, they are interested in understanding the highest level of transcendence.

Actually, this frustration with the material world is often one of the amazing qualities that brings a person into devotional service. Sometimes, a person just does not fit in or is considered dysfunctional according to the so-called normal standards of material society. Although this inability to comfortably function in the material world may appear as a disqualification to the expert materialist, it can actually act as a catalyst by pushing the person closer to devotional service and to God. However, it is unfortunate for the person and the devotional community if the person ultimately does not connect more deeply with transcendence because the dysfunctional qualities that caused him or her to feel or possibly act inappropriately in the material world can also cause him or her to remain dysfunctional in the devotee community.

In a spiritual community, devotees of the Lord definitely have certain social and spiritual etiquettes as well as specific requirements. Though we might have enough *sukrti* or pious credits to move towards God, our progress could stop at this initial level if we do not sincerely work on ourselves. Disgust, disappointment, and intense anxieties may help in bringing many to seek the Lord's shelter, but if the seekers do not fellowship properly or have their expectations fulfilled, they will develop even greater grief and depression.

Many seekers of God who came to devotional life felt such a disturbance with their environment that they even contemplated suicide. They deeply felt that life must have a higher purpose, but since they could not find or experience this higher meaning, they considered life to be meaningless and did not want to stay around. In past workshops and at temples in Europe, Africa, Australia, Malaysia, Russia, and America, when I ask how many members of the audience have contemplated suicide at some point, almost one-third of the devotees in each class raised their hands. Either they thought about suicide or had plans to follow through. In a few cases, some were about to commit suicide when they saw the devotees or noticed a spiritual book on the shelf that seemed to jump out at them. Others had dreams in which they saw devotees or their present spiritual mentor, and then the next day, they actually physically saw the devotees, or had some other powerful dream experience manifest.

Sometimes the circumstances are so dynamic that God personally intervenes just as the person prepares to end their life. This sometimes happens because the level of intensity in a person's consciousness invites the Supreme Lord to intervene. It is not the contemplation of suicide that elicits God's connection but it is the frustration, intensity, and determination. Some of us remember a certain point in our lives when we just prayed and cried intensely for help or guidance, and then the Lord seemed to come forward more, and this led to a shift in our lives. He was always there, but our intensity moved us closer to the help that He was already providing.

An unfortunate incident occurred many years ago in relation to this topic in one *asrama* in America around 1969. A new devotee named Bhakta Steve began to come to the temple in New York City. Although he was rather unusual and a little offensive, he was trying to practice *bhakti-yoga*. However, at some point, Bhakta Steve stopped coming. Srila Prabhupada, the *guru* and founder, noticed and inquired from his devoted students, "Where is Bhakta Steve?" One of the devotees explained to Srila Prabhupada that Bhakta Steve had committed suicide. Prabhupada then became very grave and tearful. He started speaking aloud in a prayerful state addressing the Lord. He said, "Dear Krishna, wherever this boy is, please let him immediately come back in a family of a devotee." He also said that Krishna sent them a soul to care for but they had not given sufficient care. Therefore, this entity experiencing such frustration in all environments, both secular as well as spiritual, took his own life.[14]

Sometimes people come into the devotional community because of their troubles with regular secular life. However, if they find that the devotional community is not sufficiently supportive, they will feel, "I am suffering in material life and now I am trying to take shelter of godly people but even here I see so much arguing, politics, hypocrisy, and impersonalism. The person may leave the environment or want to commit suicide. When someone leaves the environment, it is most unfortunate because once a person has had a connection with transcendental knowledge, his or her life will never be the same. When devotees leave their spiritual connections, they become almost like ghosts because they will not feel satisfied with the mundane materialists and they also do not feel satisfied with the spiritualists. It is as if the person has no identity. We should not wish that situation on anyone; therefore, we have a responsibility to try to create an environment in which people feel good about their devotional commitments and can make advancement. And when they do have problems, hopefully those in their environment can help bring them out of their particular problem.

Types of Depression

The different types of depression usually include unipolar and bipolar, although bipolar is sometimes confused with unipolar. Unipolar depression occurs when someone feels seriously unmotivated and full of sadness, emptiness, and distress for months and even years. Such a person feels hopeless and sees no way to get out of their misery. They often lose their desire to eat, talk, socialize, or even bathe. Some people have fallen into such deep states of depression that they will stay in a dark room for months or not take a bath for weeks. Some of us have known people who have gone through those states. Even in our own lives, when we undergo a seemingly negative situation, we may feel so miserable that nothing seems to give us pleasure. We have all had these low ebbs. A death in the family, a divorce, or a serious illness can all lead to states of depression. These are very traumatic periods, and, as a matter of fact, many people who develop cancer do so after such traumatic events in their lives such as a death, divorce, or loss of a job because the mind continuously sends distressful and aggressive messages to the organs of the body.

A person with bipolar or manic depression has a dual nature. In this condition, people will fall into such a deep depression that nothing seems capable of getting them out or stimulating them. However, they will at other times shift into sudden manic states in which they do not sleep, become excessively active, and have grandiose feelings. Some people with this condition even go days without sleeping due to this manic tendency. We might know of people who have had this experience or maybe we had it ourselves. Actually, millions of people experience these intense mental states already, and in the next ten to fifteen years, these mental challenges will increase at a drastic rate. People are having more trouble dealing with the material energy and disappointments in their lives.

Causes of Depression

Psychosomatic Illnesses

We want to look at psychosomatic illnesses, which distinctly develop from the mind. In certain instances, a person's mind literally causes them to experience a disease or causes them to repress the symptoms of a particular type of sickness, even to the degree of paralysis. Psychoneuroimmunology is a medical and psychological science, which studies the influence of the mind on the body.[15] What does this topic have to do with depression? Actually, psychosomatic illnesses illustrate the power of the mind and are important for us as we try to understand depression. Actually, as spiritualists, we already have a deep understanding of the workings of the mind. Even Arjuna, in the *Bhagavad-gita*, acknowledged that controlling the mind is more difficult than controlling the wind. We understand the process of thinking, feeling, and willing which leads to action.

If we repeatedly maintain certain thoughts in our minds, they will eventually turn into words and then actions.

The mind is always engaged in *sankalpa* and *vikalpa* or acceptance and rejection. Just as a vacuum cleaner picks up the dust on the floor, the mind also has this tendency. Sometimes it will pick up other people's thoughts and sometimes it will pick up characteristics or reflections from the environment. Every environment has a different type of atmosphere. A bar, an office, a church, or a temple all have distinct atmospheres because the thoughts of people project certain conscious and unconscious elements into the atmosphere. Some of these environments will even leave us feeling drained after prolonged association but some environments will uplift us.

The placebo effect also helps us understand the influence of the mind. Anytime doctors or researchers test a medicine, they must always test it in conjunction with the placebo effect. This means that when a group of people participates in a study to test a new medicine, some will receive the actual medication and others will receive an imitation pill. Then the doctors evaluate the people who take the genuine medicine as well as those who receive the fake pill. Interestingly, many people who receive the imitation pill actually improve. Of course, this information bewildered many doctors but now it is understood that the release of endorphins provides one explanation for this improvement. Endorphins are chemicals in the body that act as natural mood elevators and painkillers. A person's thoughts can trigger the release of these chemicals, thus influencing the physical body. The placebo effect is not just an imaginary concoction. Since people think they are taking medication, the mind influences the body to release endorphins and genuinely help improve the person's condition.

Some years ago, I spoke at the yearly convention of the

National American Medical Association and discussed how the neurotransmitters send messages throughout the body. When we feel alienated or unloved, it affects the mind. More specifically, it activates the neurotransmitters, which then send messages throughout the whole body and consequently cause an attack on the cells and organs in our bodies. Many diseases actually develop due to the mind's frequent attacks on the cells and organs in the body. The mind has that kind of power.

Conversely, when a person feels cared for and loved, their physical and psychological immune systems actually get stronger. Love literally heals, protects, and gives longevity, and a lack of love literally kills. When someone feels alienated or unloved, they may fall into a depression or carry around some type of neurosis and psychosis. Many times the person will begin to experience various physical ailments that correspond to the mental state.

Since 1995, the Harvard Medical School has annually held conferences focusing on spirituality and healing in medicine, which has drawn over 2000 health professionals annually to discuss issues relating to both the mind and body. Such conferences indicate the increasing recognition that health professionals are giving to the mind's influence on the body. Research continues to show that those people who maintain a sense of spirituality heal much better. Not only do they seem to have fewer ongoing mental challenges, but they also seem to exhibit many physiological benefits such as longevity.[16] Of course, some people claim it helps simply because the practitioners believe that it will help them. In these cases, even if one believes it works, it will work. Therefore, even on the material level, a healthy sense of spirituality has emotional and psychological benefits, what to speak of its ultimate spiritual benefits.

Heredity

When someone has an alcoholic in the family or a relative who suffers from a mental illness, that person will have a greater chance of also suffering from the same problem. The children of such individuals may develop these addictions or mental challenges since some of the problems seem to have a connection with the genes. Even though a person with this background might try to practice as a spiritualist, they will more than likely still be affected due to hereditary influences. For example, a person whose parents suffer from depression will be three times more likely to have the same problems.[17] Children of alcoholics also have a greater tendency to develop an addiction to alcohol, have poor relationships, or end up as runaways.

Biological Factors

Sometimes talk therapy can help a person deal with different types of depression and mental disturbances but not always. In some cases, such verbal guidance and counseling by a trained therapist can help the patient refocus and gradually work through their problems. Other types of mental illness as well as depression actually have a biological origin. There are many different types of ailments, diseases, or problems that can cause a mental disturbance. Sometimes a physical imbalance such as sugar diabetes or low blood sugar can lead to an imbalanced mental state. A lack of certain vitamins or nutrients can create problems, even a thyroid problem. Some studies suggest that many people in mental institutions actually have a biological problem.

Maternity Blues

Women often experience postnatal depression, which some

specialists refer to as the maternity blues. This type of depression affects fifty percent of women during the ten days immediately following childbirth and fifteen percent suffer from the blues within six weeks of childbirth. Within the two weeks following the delivery of a baby, women have a greater likelihood than at any other time of being admitted to a psychiatric hospital. During this time following childbirth, women might experience great anxiety and fear about the baby, feelings of inadequacy as a mother, irritability, guilt, and a loss of libido. This is also a time in which some will feel increased phobic symptoms and even suicidal thoughts.[18]

CEO Depression

Depression among CEOs, or executives with the primary decision-making authority in a corporation or organization, is another serious area creating problems for some of the most successful people in the world. Even managers of the top Fortune 500 companies in the United States suffer from chronic depression while trying to run their corporations. Consequently, many have stepped down from such positions or undergone constant therapy while others have unfortunately even committed suicide.

Philip J. Burguieres, a CEO of a top Fortune 500 company who had to undergo therapy for chronic depression, explains in the magazine *Psychology Today*, "At some point in their careers, fully 25 percent of top level executives go through a severe depression. You would be shocked at the number of CEOs, now running big companies, who are suicidally depressed."[19] They have found that reaching the top and being crowned the king is in itself the problem. The journey to the top was the actual fun part. After arriving at that point, not only is the mystery and adventure gone, but many also find that this ultimate position has not given them the anticipated satisfaction and happiness. Of course, the goal has been a big letdown. Many do not feel good about themselves and find themselves facing terrible relationships with their colleagues, employees, and most unfortunately with their own family members.

The article mentions how successful corporate executives may be more vulnerable to depression—more than the general population—due to forces within as well as without. Sometimes the very qualities that helped the executive rise to the top stem from an extremely dark part of his or her consciousness. Burguieres himself says, "There are two kinds of managers. Those who are successful because they're aggressive and goal-oriented, and those who are successful because they fear being unsuccessful."[20]

The author of the article, Hara Estroff Marano, lists several reasons that contribute to the risk of depression in successful executives:

1. **A stressful job**—Some CEOs have thousands and, in some cases, hundreds of thousands of employees and stockholders. They have to make serious decisions that will affect the lives of many people.

2. **Many CEOs live a very isolated life**—It can be very lonely at the top. Some have been responsible for their own isolation because they are not only CEOs but also chairmen of the board.

3. **Material success is often a disappointment**—Since we are actually spiritual entities who have a material body, profession, car, home, and so on, we can never attain full happiness only by nourishing our physical existence. The

illusion that we will be fully satisfied once we have more material success always tricks us. For many people, the challenge and anticipation of success is more exciting than actually reaching the goal. Once they reach the top, they will normally have to confront their illusions.

4. **Hardcore success often comes at the cost of intimate relationships**—Many successful CEOs work extremely hard and, by the time many have been able to attain their highest dreams of material success, they have fractured their marital and family relationships if not completely destroying them.

5. **Those at the top try to mask their problems**—Such depressed executives try to take shelter of illicit affairs, intoxications, and so on. They self-medicate themselves and engage in a promiscuous life, desperately hunting for the happiness and pleasure that has eluded them.

6. **The most successful executives are not so easy to treat**—These executives have expertly played the game of posturing and looking good. They can be excellent controllers; good at hiding what really lurks within their consciousness; intimidating; arrogant; and sometimes even dishonest. For these reasons, it may be more difficult for the therapist to encourage such so-called "successful people" to really move outside of their artificial fortresses.[21]

Due to the pervasiveness of depression, some experts refer to it as the common cold of psychiatry. We see a powerful dilemma in this case. Many people who have been failures or who have not accomplished their goals feel extremely frustrated, depressed, and even suicidal. On the other hand, many who have accomplished their goals feel even more disappointed and depressed after succeeding. If we have external wealth but remain internally bankrupt, we will ultimately feel miserable and see life through the eyes of disappointment, frustration, sadness, and gloom with seemingly little to look forward to in the future.

The Dark Night of the Soul

Christian theology has a term called "the dark night of the soul" originally coined by a 16th century Spanish saint know as Saint John of the Cross. He describes this dark night as a period of serious testing for all seekers on the spiritual path. At certain times during our spiritual progression, we may go through periods of rapid advancement and growth although we may find it hard to perceive the situation in this positive way. We might reach a point in our lives when we begin to think, "I am chanting; meditating; praying; fasting; reading the scriptures; visiting the temple, church, synagogue, or mosque; and following the spiritual laws and principles, but I am miserable! Where is God?" At this point, the person even begins to seriously doubt God's mercy and attentiveness. Such a person might feel that even God has forsaken them.

We can look at this situation in a more graphic way because our advancement is not necessarily vertical. We normally advance but then work through certain challenges at a particular level until we make advancement to the next level. Sometimes we must face certain obstacles that take time to work through and consequently, we feel stagnant. We may even feel that God Himself is not protecting us. However, at such times, the Lord is actually ready to elevate our consciousness and bring us closer to Him so He gives us certain obstacles or blocks in our lives that we have to transcend. He may give us problems as a way to speed up our evolution so that we can more quickly burn up negative reactions and move forward more expediently.

Saint John explains that this dark night of the soul manifests as a type of internal dryness or aridity. When a spiritual seeker first embarks on the spiritual path, he or she often experiences an initial taste and excitement for the prayers, rituals, songs, and dances associated with the worship of God. However, this initial joy often stems from pride or self-centeredness that Srila Visvanatha Cakravarti refers to as *utsahamayi* or sudden enthusiasm. However, after a period of time, the Lord wants to help His devotee become more genuine so He takes away this initial false pleasure, leaving the devotee in a state of internal dryness and without any taste. Saint John explains that very few souls actually make it through this test because, as soon as this so-called spiritual excitement dwindles, most people run back to material pleasures. However, if we understand the purpose of this dark night, we will feel excited at the very thought of transcending so many of our old patterns and limitations.

The dark night of the soul can lead to depression if a person does not understand the reasons for it, but the dark night is not an ordinary depression. Although its symptoms may mirror depression, Saint John makes a distinction between ordinary depression and the dark night of the soul. It is actually an arrangement made by the Lord Himself to help a person with deep faith and determination to go deeper. Depression, on the other hand, may just result from excessive attachment, lack of faith, laziness, and so on. The dark night of the soul is an extraordinary opportunity for the faithful soul rather than a demoralizing depression.

Reflect on a time in your own spiritual j
you felt abandoned by God. Although you
way, you later found out that not only had Go
you, but He was actually giving you some spec... ...., ...,
that time. We often experience depression or anxiety when we
feel that the Lord has abandoned us or when we cannot understand the events in our lives. If you look back through your life,
you may even recall times when you have in fact experienced
such a period and began to question God's existence or His
fairness. However, when you look back now, you realize the
purpose of such events because they helped you elevate your
consciousness. Often, the result of intense suffering is eleva-
tion in consciousness. Such suffering gives us the intensity to
break through the last layers of mundane consciousness.[22]

The Influence of Subtle Entities

As more and more people engage in sinful rituals and allow
their lust to increase, they actually invite more negative influences. Mundane music and sound vibrations also make them
susceptible to more negative influences. Therefore, individuals
who are not becoming more spiritual are gradually losing some
of their free will and their creative expression of consciousness. The bombardments of different types of influences and
propaganda will have a greater affect on them.

We sometimes hear about a criminal who has killed dozens
of people and who might even commit the most nefarious acts
such as cutting up people's body parts. Such people who we
might refer to as serial killers are not ordinary criminals, since
they viciously attack people one after another in such heinous
ways. They enjoy taking life and seeing people suffer. In some
of these cases, they have literally been possessed and their
minds have been overtaken. In other cases, different subtle

entities affect the body and their thoughts, desires, and activities are so degraded and low that they invite or allow very negative and sinister entities to enter into their bodies and influence them to partake in extremely negative activities. These increasing phenomena also can cause mental illness and depression. Some people who suffer from schizophrenia or mental disturbances have had their active consciousness pushed aside by the presence or influence of a ghost. Such ghosts or disembodied entities are always looking for a vehicle to possess.

Women More Prone to Depression

Women usually suffer from depression more than men and have a greater susceptibility to fall into states of depression. One reason is that many women feel that they have less control of their environments and tend to approach situations from a more emotional perspective. When a person has issues such as economic, political, social, or religious problems, it will affect them a little less if they feel some sense of control of the situation. However, when a person finds him or herself in the middle of a problem and must simply remain at the mercy of the situation, it causes far more stress on the consciousness.

Menopause also affects a woman, and although both men and woman go through a type of menopause, it more distinctly affects the woman. Men also go through various cycles just as the mind goes through various cycles. Men usually go through one of the best times in their lives when their children grow up and leave the family. After raising the children, fathers feel happy to see their daughters or sons go off to college or find a job and a spouse. However, this period of life might depress a woman more than any other time in her life. She feels that she has done so much and has offered her life to take care of the family so she begins to wonder if anyone even thinks about her anymore. The man feels a sense of relief but the woman really needs to feel appreciated at this time in her life.

The World Health Organization reports that 20% of the world's female population has been physically or sexually abused by a man at some time in their life. Furthermore, investigations suggest that 14% to 20% of women in the United States will be raped once in their lifetime.[23] If a woman has repressed certain aspects of her past, these memories may begin to surface between her late thirties and forties, and this can lead to some disturbances in the mind or consciousness. The man may not understand the woman's struggles during this period since some of her problems stem from issues of abuse during her childhood.

When a girl reaches her early twenties, she may also experience a level of depression because of the transition into a different stage in her life. Although she is no longer a teenager, she still may not have much control over her situation. When people find themselves in that predicament, they should not become overly distracted because most will pass through this phase. As we embrace our spiritual life more deeply, we will find relief from such impediments. Furthermore, many of the submissions throughout this book can surely help one understand, minimize, and transcend these difficulties. When a man sees his wife or daughters undergoing these challenges, he must try to understand and remain compassionate to their unique struggles.

Misuse of ancient cultures is another serious area that leads to problems and facilitates depression. At the International Women's Conference held in Beijing, China in 1995, reports indicate that Indian and African women are among the most abused on the planet in terms of battery. More reports also reveal that, in many Muslim communities, women suffer from extensive abuse and battery. Cultures that adhere to the idea that the man provides and dominates in a monarchal or autocratic arrangement can become very destructive if the people abuse this philosophy. Instead of caretaking and facilitating the women, the men can create a completely opposite situation, which then leads to various types of abuse. When this happens, it of course produces great depression among the women. In many cases, the men just accept the arrangement as traditional culture without thinking deeply on the matter or feeling at fault. Unfortunately, the abusers justify their actions with so-called religious doctrines. In such cases, people use religions, which are supposed to guarantee the strong protection of women, to manipulate and exploit them.

Lord Caitanya, Srila Bhaktisiddhanta, and Srila Prabhupada himself were all against excessive body consciousness, which manifests as racism, castism, brahmanism, and sahajiyaism. Castism is a belief in social hierarchy based on birth in a particular family. Brahmanism is the idea that only those born in families of *brahmanas* are actually qualified to serve as priests. Sahajiyaism refers to people who are presumptuous and artificial in their spiritual expressions. These distortions of Vedic culture can cause spousal abuse and improper care of women. It can cause the men to dominate in an unhealthy way, which produces depression, dysfunctional patterns, and distress. Too much stress also has ways of affecting the physical body, leading to disease. Many women on the planet are experiencing cancer, heart disease, or diabetes due to problems within the family that create stress in the mind and affect the physical body. This often results from the exploitation and abuse of women justified by an improper understanding of ancient cultures and religions.

These points are important for us as spiritualists because

we want to always honor each other as devotees of God. If you are married, you are not just with your own husband, wife, or children but you are with servants of God. You are with a partner in order to work together in the service of the Lord. Ideally, the husband should see his wife as a gift from God rather than just as his own wife or possession. Similarly, the wife should see the husband as a gift from Krishna as well. Both the husband and wife should see their children as gifts rather than just as their own children or possessions.

If we only see our family members as our property, we will not give them sufficient love and care because people tend to feel justified in ignoring, cheating on, beating, or battering their property because after all, they can treat their own property however they like. If they want to deny or cheat on their property, they simply act according to their whims because, after all, they own the object. However, if we understand that the property belongs to God and we merely caretake on His behalf, we want to relate to each other in a way that will please the actual owner. Therefore, in our relationships, we should try to relate to our wife, husband, or children in a way that will please the real owner. In this way, we will be able to avoid so much of the distress that brings physical ailments, mental disturbances, and frustration and that minimizes and distorts ancient culture and religion.

Although women go through all of this pain and distress, their life expectancies range from five to eight years longer than men.[24] First of all, it shows that women have remarkable strength to survive all of these abuses and still outlive the men. It also means that many women will take care of their husbands in their last years and will even bury or cremate them. Considering this point, men should remember that what goes around comes around because this can be an excellent time for some women to get back at their abusive fathers, uncles, husbands, and so on. Actually, some of these men will return in their next lives in the bodies of women and will then suffer from abuse. Actually, if women, children, *brahmanas*, elders, and cows do not receive proper care, the length of one's life span will decrease (*Srimad-Bhagavatam* 1.8.5, purport). Maybe this explains the decrease in men's life spans.

Healthy Ways to Cope with Depression

Spiritually Minded Therapists

We now want to spend some time looking at solutions or at least ways of dealing with depression in a healthy manner. First of all, we have a need for spiritually minded therapists or therapists who are appreciative of the spiritual culture and most importantly, who are actually following such a culture. Although some of these mental challenges are physiological or biological, other mental disturbances stem from the mind, which means that talk therapy can help a person work through them. However, it can be dangerous to go to a therapist who does not understand or appreciate the spiritual dimension because they can make our situation even worse.

For instance, when a saintly person starts speaking in a spirit of humility, the average therapist will categorize and begin to treat the problem as low self-esteem. They do not understand that humility is a part of the wealth of a saintly person. The saint's gratitude and closeness to God ultimately make him or her humble. The aspiring spiritualist may be fixed in simplicity and renunciation, but the therapist may see this as anti-social behavior. The saint may be pursuing chastity or celibacy, but the therapist may see this as unhealthy sexual repression. The list goes on and on. For these reasons, there is a need to have godly devotees with special expertise so that they can service their own communities and keep the devotional focus.

Maintain Body and Soul Together

We sometimes think that we can solve all of our problems simply through the execution of the rituals, and actually such practices can provide the essential help if we perform them with sufficient depth and purity. However, since such depth is very rare, additional help is needed to assist the practitioner in the removal of various blocks. This is one of the main reasons we are offering this book to the international community. We especially want to help aspiring transcendentalists obtain better results in their practices and gain better control of the mind by eradicating its enemies. As spiritual institutions and communities expand all around the world, we need to maintain body and soul together. The Vaisnava saint Bhaktivinoda Thakura explained that, in order to develop a healthy community, we must balance the following four needs:

• We need to take care of the body.

• We need to properly stimulate the mind.

• We need to have a sense of social well-being.

• We need to study spiritual texts.[25]

As we embark on the devotional path and experience the challenges that go along with normal association, we should also seek out help, and if possible, search for those in the community who have a little more understanding of the physical and psychological needs as well as the spiritual aspects.

The Enemies of the Mind

Imagine a situation in which six enemies constantly surround you and incessantly wait for the opportune moment to attack when you put your guard down. As soon as you become lackadaisical, they will swiftly approach. However, we can try to sufficiently reinforce ourselves and strengthen our weak spots, knowing that *maya* will attack us in these weak areas. The six enemies are lust, anger, greed, bewilderment, intoxication, and envy. These are some of the ways in which depression, anxiety, gloom, and frustration affect the mind. If we know the enemy's hiding place, we can keep our distance instead of remaining in an insecure position or allowing the enemy to constantly ambush us. The enemies of course hide in the mind.

Many mental breakdowns deal with the mindset of lust because unsatisfied lust turns into anger and then turns into great illusion and confusion. For some people, it even causes them to experience neurosis, psychosis, schizophrenia, and so on. However, some people experience so much anger that it turns into hypertension, ulcers, physical diseases, and even violence to others or themselves. We can also understand depression as anger turned toward oneself. In our discussion on anger, we already acknowledged that anger always has a victim, either others or ourselves. People often cannot keep a balance between their intellect and their mind; consequently, they have ongoing mental challenges that may last for the rest of their lives.

Enviousness also creates an imbalance within us. We should be *param-duhkha-duhkhi-kripam-buddhi* which means that we should feel the misery of others as well as their happiness. We should feel happy for another person when we see something positive happen in their life. Actually, we should feel the same happiness for them that we would feel for our own selves in that same situation. This type of mindset can help prevent depression and mental disturbance. If we learn how to weed out negative tendencies, we will find that it will lead to some wonderful solutions.

Relinquish Selfishness

If we find ourselves in a state of depression, we can also examine our degree of self-centeredness or selfishness. There are two ways to play God. We play God when we see ourselves as superior and as the most important person. We also play God when we place ourselves in the center by thinking of ourselves as the most inferior or most unfortunate person. Other times people play God by considering that everything revolves around their problems. If you ask them, "How are you?" they will respond, "I am so glad you asked! I have a headache, stomachache, and a pain in my leg. I need a raise and my son is giving me such problems." However, if we focus too much on our misfortunes, it will reinforce our problems rather than eliminate them. Selflessness is one way of decreasing our problems. If we try to help someone else or try to go beyond our own immediate situation, we will see that God will give us the help we need and even take away our own particular issues.

For instance, if you manage an institutional corporation and you see an employee doing well, you will give them even more facility to increase their work. If someone is not doing such a nice job, you call them out and maybe even withdraw them from their position. Similarly, when God sees a devotee trying to work hard on His behalf, He will then remove any obstacles so that the person can serve better. Rather than just focusing on the obstacles, we should proactively try to find ways to increase our quality of service. Krishna promises that He will maintain what we have and carry what we lack.

ananyas cintayanto mam
ye janah paryupasate
tesam nityabhiyuktanam
yoga-ksemam vahamy aham

But those who always worship Me with
exclusive devotion, meditating on My
transcendental form—to them I carry
what they lack, and I preserve what
they have.
Bhagavad-gita 9.22

He has made this promise and He will fulfill it.

Depression means that **we are focusing too much on
our own problems and withholding our love from others**.
However, as we give more love to others, we will never have
a shortage of love coming to us. This is the nature of *karma*. If
we wait for others to care for us and love us, we will remain in a
state of impoverishment. However, as we try to extend our service and love, we will find that the depression will decrease.

Forgiveness and Mindfulness

Depression also results from a lack of forgiveness.
Sometimes people have genuine issues but they have not yet
forgiven another person. As we said earlier, the mind affects the
body, and anger can even cause the body to attack its own cells.
Mindfulness is another beneficial practice that can help free us
of depression and mental challenges. It will help us constantly
reflect at all times on God who makes all of these arrangements
for us. It will also help us see how the Lord has already come
forward at a difficult time. Then, when we go through another
difficult period, we will be able to remember the previous help

He gave us, and we will have faith that He can help us even more in the future.

Faith is Most Important

We will not have the ability to persevere without faith but we cannot fake faith. When certain aspects of a person's life are not going so well, his or her faith does get weaker. Our faith relates to what has happened in the past; what is happening in the present; and more directly with what we are anticipating in the future. If our past has been rough and our present is incoherent, our faith in the future will be weak. However, if we see positive events around us that we feel good about, we will have strong faith. Only a rare person can maintain strong faith when they have had a difficult past and a rocky present. In our communities, we want to create environments that will energize us and help increase our faith.

Gratitude as a Way of Life

Sometimes our mental challenges become very stagnant because we do not move through them, and we do not appreciate the past. The more we have gratitude, the more we create auspiciousness in the future. Sometimes the Supreme Personality of Godhead gives to us and sometimes He takes away. As devotees, we want to have such a grateful mindset that when God gives us wealth, we say thank you. When God takes it away and puts us into a state of impoverishment, we thank Him for protecting us from false pride. We thank Him for any situation that allows us to keep a simple life. When God gives us good health, we can say, "Thank you Lord for Your kindness because You know how much I hate pain! You have given me such a nice, healthy body so that I can serve You because You know that if I have too much pain, I will simply blaspheme." If

God gives us sickness or pain, then we say, "Thank you Lord for putting me in this state so that I can be more contemplative. It will help me appreciate good health and give me a chance to slow down so that I can read more." If God makes us famous, we can say, "Thank you Lord because you know how much I need my ego stimulated. Thank you for helping me so that I can be a good devotee in the midst of all this fame." When God makes us infamous, we can still say, "Thank you Lord for making me very humble. You have put me into a situation so that I will not think of myself as the proprietor or controller."

If we can just develop this consciousness and constantly thank the Supreme in any situation, we will be able to learn and grow from any circumstance. We will make the auspicious situations more auspicious and we will turn any inauspicious situations into auspicious ones. It will become a learning experience, and as we honor it with gratitude, Krishna will naturally make arrangements for us.

Importance of Attitude

The mind is the greatest enemy although we can make it our greatest friend. It all depends on attitude. We want to develop humility, not low self-esteem. Rupa Gosvami and many other great *acaryas* have all mentioned the importance of humility but it does not mean that we should have low self-esteem. It means that we should have such a high esteem for the spiritual teachers, scriptures, and the Supreme Lord that we feel awed by their appreciation for the higher spiritual reality. The closer we come to the Supreme Lord, the more we advance. The more we see the magnanimous nature, beauty, and ability of God, the more it will humble us. As we genuinely advance, we receive more from the Lord but we will simultaneously feel more humble. We will realize that the Supreme Lord gives us far more than our actual quality. We literally become more humble due to contact with such greatness.

The *Srimad-Bhagavatam* 10.14.8 mentions that one should have faith in spite of suffering due to the experiences of past *karma*. "My dear Lord, one who earnestly waits for You to bestow Your causeless mercy upon him, all the while patiently suffering the reactions of his past misdeeds and offering You respectful obeisances with his heart, words and body, is surely eligible for liberation, for it has become his rightful claim." Srila Sridhara Swami explains the concept of *daya-bhak* in his commentary on this verse. "Just as a legitimate son has to simply remain alive to gain an inheritance from his father, one who simply remains alive in Krishna consciousness, following the regulative principles of *bhakti-yoga*, automatically becomes eligible to receive the mercy of the Personality of Godhead. In other words, he will be promoted to the Kingdom of God" (*Srimad-Bhagavatam* 10.14.8, purport). Basically, the father has written a will that includes the son or daughter as inheritors. In order to receive their inheritance, they simply have to remain alive. It is already arranged and legally organized if they simply stay alive.

Sridhara Swami tells us this truth. If we simply maintain our *sadhana* and continue with our devotion in spite of the many setbacks and challenges, we can return to the spiritual world. Setbacks happen in institutions, families, and to us individually but we just have to avoid getting too depressed, discouraged, and disappointed. We should try to thank the Lord and try to learn from the circumstances. We wait for the Supreme to do better than we could have done for ourselves. This means that we need steady faith and perseverance. We can all encourage each other by first trying to have that faith and that faith will spill over and help someone else. In this way, we all inherit the Kingdom of God.

Helping Others

Some of you may work in institutions in which the people suffer from schizophrenia, neurosis, psychosis, or depression. As we said, some of them are possessed and some are just so stressed out by the enemies of the mind. What can we do to help such people? First, if necessary, we must see that they get relevant understanding and professional help. In some cases, we can also help some people the best simply by offering them *prasadam* (spiritually blessed food) or by letting them constantly hear the holy names of God.

In other cases, we can help a person through our own devotion, especially our relatives. By engaging in our spiritual practices, they will get some credit. Just by having a devotee in the family, even previous generations will benefit. Srila Bhaktisiddhanta states, "When a great saint, a pure devotee appears in a family, then his ancestors and descendants for a hundred generations each are elevated. When a devotee of the middle stature (*madhyama bhagavata*) appears in a family, then his ancestors and descendants for fourteen generations each are elevated. When a neophyte devotee appears in a family, then his ancestors and descendents for three generations each are elevated."[26] If someone in our family suffers from depression or even a serious mental disturbance, we can help them by intensifying our own devotion.

We can also talk with them and help free them of some of their attachments because an excessive focus on their own problem has actually led them into their particular mental crisis. We can also help them develop more gratitude and give more love that will then shelter them. Sometimes we have to help them understand the "pay offs." Some people maintain their depression because of what they seemingly get in return. For instance, they want sympathy; they use it as an excuse to not make themselves more available; they want attention from others; or they use it as a reason to quit their jobs. Others hide behind the depression to cover up other problems. Most times, these pay offs are deeply unconscious.

Possession also happens due to the lowness of a person's consciousness since it attracts the presence of such a being. As the person raises their consciousness, such entities will not remain in the environment because they will not be able to connect with the person. Just as filth attracts rats and insects, a low consciousness will attract certain entities. However, as we intensify our consciousness through devotional reflections, it will create some barriers of psychic and spiritual protection. As mental illness increases, we will all need more protection from the environment for ourselves and for our families. We can get that protection through strong *sadhana* or spiritual practices and association.

Thirty-Two Ways to Cope with Depression

I would like to end this discussion on depression by listing thirty-two areas that can help one in coping with this problem. I also want to give a few distinct items that can assist in depression associated with panic attacks in adults as well as in children. Most of these points have already been addressed in this section but we will include several new points in order to broaden our understanding of ways to help ourselves and to help others who are struggling with this great obstacle.

1. **Medication**—Depression is physical as well as psychological, and chronic depression can prevent the brain from releasing healthy hormones. Therefore, medication is often necessary to help people strengthen themselves which can then enable them to receive further treatments

and support, ultimately freeing themselves from both the medication and depression.

2. **Understand Why a Person Tries to Surrender to God**—Most people approach the Godhead out of distress or material exhaustion.

3. **Understand the Mind Better**—Recognize the power of psychosomatic influences on the body and become more aware of the effects of neurosis and psychosis. Remind ourselves of the mind's position as the best friend or greatest enemy.

4. **Understand the Difference between Experiencing Failure and Being a Failure**—Making a temporary mistake is far different from being a failure.

5. **Understand Unipolar Versus Bipolar Depression**—Recognize how depression can manifest as lower states of consciousness as well as in grandiose delusions.

6. **More Light**—Since some depression may stem from the environment, having brighter lights and experiencing more sun will help. There is seasonal depression that is associated with bad weather.

7. **Thyroid**—For some people, their depression is due to thyroid difficulties. Proper medication can assist.

8. **Chemical Imbalance**—Good therapists will be able to evaluate whether the cause of the depression stems from a chemical imbalance or a psychological problem.

9. **Exercise and Diet**—Exercise produces endorphins. The diet should be free of chocolate, caffeine, alcohol, and meat. All of these complicate the depression.

10. **Stress Reduction Techniques**—Meditation, visualizations, affirmations, and massage can help.

11. **Journaling**—Writing is a very powerful way to gain more control of one's mental powers.

12. **Be More Assertive**—Holding too many emotions within can act as a catalyst for depression.

13. **Put an End to "What If" Fearing**—Instead of thinking and fearing about what can go wrong, think about what can go right.

14. **Anger Management**—A mind that is too disturbed will remain enslaved by depression.

15. **Practice Forgiveness**—When we forgive, we let go of many anxieties.

16. **Heredity**—If depression has been in our families, we must give extra attention to ourselves so that we will not become carriers of the same problems.

17. **Defend Against Possession**—If we can avoid lower consciousness, we can protect ourselves from such intrusions.

18. **Good Sadhana (Spiritual Practices)**—If we are regu-

lated in our spiritual practices, the mind is less susceptible to attacks.

19. **Raising Our Spiritual Standards**—As we become more devoted, those karmically connected with us will benefit as well as ourselves.

20. **Prayer and Chanting**—If we call on God's names more seriously, we will get quicker relief.

21. **Honoring Blessed Food (Prasadam)**—Taking sanctified water or food will help to raise our consciousness.

22. **Understand the Dark Night of the Soul**—Be eager to honor this state of severe challenges as a blessing for growth.

23. **Understanding Maternity Blues**—To avoid being overwhelmed, women can anticipate some bewilderment and depression a short time after childbirth and prepare themselves accordingly.

24. **Understanding CEO Depression**—Understand that material success has its own problems. It can even take the mystery and adventure out of life, especially if one has not developed a rich inner life.

25. **Avoid Excessive Attachments**—Extreme attachments are one of the most serious problems that bring on and maintain depression.

26. **Gratitude as a Way of Life**—If we are filled with grati-

tude, we will not have any room left to host depression.

27. **Be More Selfless**—Depression is a sign that we are too self-centered.

28. **Positive Internal Dialogue**—We are more what we think and tell ourselves than what we say or do.

29. **Depression is a Lack of Sending Out Sufficient Love**—When we stop worrying so much about ourselves, stop waiting for others to support or love us, and stop holding back our own love, we will check our depression. Those who send out abundant love will never have a shortage.

30. **Short-Term Goals**—Having successful short-term goals will help us with the ultimate victory.

31. **Pay Offs**—We must try to understand what subconscious rewards or payments we are getting for maintaining our depression.

32. **Laughter**—We must learn to laugh at our attachments, foolishness, and at our determination to engage in a drama of illusions.

Six Steps to End Panic Attacks
1. **Give Yourself Permission to Feel Anxious**—Know the situation will go away and accept the understanding that it will not kill you, because fear actually feeds the problem.

2. **Ask Yourself What is Really Bothering You at the Moment**—What exactly are your immediate scary thoughts and reflections?

3. **See it as Excitement, Not Anxiety**—Excitement is normal and natural. It is a sign of being attentive and responsive.

4. **Use Positive Self-Talk**—Whatever we internally talk about on a regular basis, we will get more of in the future.

5. **Distract Yourself**—Use the adrenaline energy to act productively. By changing our bodily activities, we change our mental activities.

6. **Learn to Laugh at Yourself**—Laughing is the topmost therapy. We will discuss this in the next chapter.

Helping Children with Anxiety and Panic Attacks

1. **Get Professional Help**—Make sure the therapist or individual understands spiritual culture.

2. **Make Yourself More Healthy**—If we are broken, how can we help fix others, especially those who depend on us?

3. **Maintain a Good Authentic Spiritual Environment**—Remember, it takes a village to raise a child.

4. **As a Parent, Don't Be Afraid to Get Help**—Parents may feel that outside help will create more anxiety for the child, cause others to categorize them as bad parents, or place labels on their children.

5. **Take Notice, If Possible, of the Event Which Brought on the Child's Trauma**—Sometimes there might be an obvious cause such as an accident, someone breaking into the house, etc.

6. **Parents Should Avoid Rushing in to Fix Everything**— This will cause the child's situation to worsen and the parent's whole life might end up centered around the child's problem. The parent can desensitize the child gently and must be careful to not reinforce the child's illusion.

7. **Encourage the Child to Talk**—Encourage them to talk in pictures and help them understand that there is no immediate threat to their safety.

8. **Back and Foot Massages**—Massages have been shown to bring about distinct improvements.

9. **Medication**—This can help if the child is being tortured with their mental challenges. Children as young as three to six years of age are now being diagnosed with depression,[27] but one should be very slow and cautious to give young children medications.

10. **Try to Eliminate White Sugar, Caffeine, and Chocolate**—They can send a child into panic attacks and stages of depression.

11. **Teach Them Self-Talk**—"It is not a big deal. It is just anxiety which will go away."

12. **Give Them Some Responsible Task**—Just as in adults, a child needs ways to free his or her mind from negative reflections.

Questions and Answers

Question: Many people do not seem to fit in properly in either the material or spiritual environment. Although they may try to practice as devotees of God, they just do not feel enthused even while engaged in the rituals or in service. At the same time, they know that they do not belong in the material world. It is a difficult situation because they do not know where they belong. They know that basic material life will not get them anywhere but spiritual life just seems too heavy. How does a person cope with that type of predicament?

Answer: In any field of activities, it is important to focus. For instance, if you go to college and switch your major every month, you will never pass the examinations. You may study medicine, engineering, law, or education for brief periods of time, but if you do not focus on a specific field, you will not accomplish much. It takes a significant amount of work. We can also compare this to spiritual life because we really have to focus and do the necessary in order to gain a stronger foundation. However, if we cannot seem to focus our attention in any one place and also have so many distracting desires, it will make the process much harder.

Question: I have found that many struggling spiritualists leave religious institutions because of financial problems but they come back when they recover. Could you comment on this topic?

Answer: An economic situation can definitely bring on departure and depression at times. In the material world, we hear the saying, "Money is the honey," which shows its significance. Yes, financial considerations are important, even in spiritual environments. An aspirant may ask, "I like the community, institution, and philosophy but how will it pay my mortgage? How will this lifestyle, commitment, or philosophy take care of my insurance? How will it pay for my children's education?"

Once again, we can refer to the four distinct needs that Bhaktivinoda Thakura lists for the individual as well as for a successful community. He did not just tell us to focus on the scripture and engage in rituals while neglecting all the other aspects of our life. First, he said that we must take care of the physical body. We are not our bodies but we must still give them sufficient care. Secondly, he states that the mind must be satisfied and stimulated in a way that will help us feel good about our projects or plans. Third, he writes about the need for a sense of social well-being which would include economic considerations. One may not necessarily want to become a millionaire but one wants to have sufficient money so that one does not have to worry about money. We want to have good health so that we do not have to worry about the body. We want sufficient commodities so that we do not have to worry about such distractions. In most cases, a person will find it easier to accept spiritual life if these basic needs are met. Finally, he talked about the importance of following and being guided by the scriptures while pursuing the other three goals.[28]

If we can balance all of these aspects of our lives, Bhaktivinoda Thakura says that we will have less depression, mental disturbances, and anxiety. We will have a more genuine institution and community because each individual will feel a greater sense of value and will give more value to the environment. As we take care of our families, it is especially important for us to have a good balance of all these necessary aspects of our lives so that we can try to organize our priorities. However, we constantly want to try to connect with the scriptures because we are spiritualists undergoing a material experience and the scriptures remind us of our higher duties.

Question: Psychologists and mental health professionals often have the conception that people take shelter of religious practices due to a weak mind. They think that religionists follow their practices because they have nothing to depend on and cannot bear the reality of material life. Could you comment on this conception that they have?

Answer: This conception often comes from the negative influence of the Western reductionist mentality. Keep in mind that much of Western scholarship stems from a materialistic paradigm. Such a paradigm does not accept life after death and sees the enjoyment of the senses as the purpose of life. Therefore, when we hear a message from someone, it is important to first examine the characteristics of the messenger. Although psychiatrists and psychologists can offer very valuable assistance, we do have to be careful for several reasons.

First of all, we must remember that psychology and psychiatry are not exact sciences. Some time ago in Michigan, USA and in Omsk, Siberia, I spoke to groups of psychiatrists and started off by tactfully challenging them. I explained that although they get paid so much money and deal with people's lives in great crises, they do not have any common understanding of what constitutes normality. How does one categorize a person as normal? Not only do they not have an actual standard, but they also have no understanding of the soul or the influences from previous lifetimes. This science is somewhat speculative.

Furthermore, some physicians suffer from mental challenges themselves, which sometimes lead them to select psychiatry as their specialty. Since some might enter into the profession for this reason, psychiatrists might also go through an analysis to gain an understanding of their own issues first in order to avoid transmitting them onto a patient. In this regard, suicide rates have been reported to be particularly high among male and female physicians and psychiatrists.[29] Reports also indicate that physicians were more likely to have poor marriages, use drugs and alcohol heavily, and obtain psychotherapy.[30] The work is stressful because it is not an exact science and it is practiced in a stressful environment. The hospital is a place of disease and people often get sick due to infections that they acquire in the institution.

We should take these points into consideration when we hear their theories. People may claim that religionists are just weak-minded, but the majority of the people making these claims are themselves weak-minded. Therefore, we might want to scrutinize before we fully embrace what they have to offer because we realize that many of the problems are *karmic*. Many of our experiences in this lifetime deal with certain issues from our past lives as well as our past in this life. We have not just come into existence with this body, but we have existed in the past. We also understand that we have a mind and we have a body, but we are the soul. At any one given moment, all of these aspects of us are interacting in various ways. Through the study of books such as the *Bhagavad-gita*, we understand the impact of lust, greed, enviousness, and so on. Therefore, we want to turn to spirituality so that we can genuinely reduce such incarcerating disturbances.

Basically, we must examine more selectively the opinions of people who have the highest rates of suicide, more divorce, and more susceptibility to drug usage. We want to find ways to help the whole self which includes the physical, emotional, and of course, the spiritual. We ultimately want to do that which will nourish the soul.

Actually, the most important variable in the course of therapy is the relationship between the doctor and the patient. In other words, the type of therapy that one uses is not always the significant factor. The most dominant variable that always seems to make a difference is the dynamic relationship. If the patient feels cared for, he or she will trust the help and guidance of the therapist to a greater extent. It shows that it deals with much more than just the externals but with *sambandha* or relationships.

Question: Why do some people think that their own ideas are best and the ideas of other people are less significant? What is the cause of this mentality?

Answer: We sometimes see that spiritual practitioners have rather sectarian views and can even be dangerous fanatics. Some religionists consider their religion to be the only way and the best path. Maybe an analogy will help. Sometimes a wife says, "No one knows how wonderful my husband is." Or a husband might say, "My wife is so wonderful. Nobody has a wife like mine. She is just perfect." We are happy to hear such expressions because it means that the person feels quite satisfied about the relationship. If we hear a person say, "My religion is so wonderful; no one has a religion like mine," we can feel happy that a person feels satisfied with their process. However, a problem begins when the husband starts saying, "No one else has a wife like mine and only she should be appreciated." When this happens, the person begins to deride another in order to build up his or her own case. When someone says that they have the best, we can think, "Let it prove itself. Let the effects show its greatness and then we can all honor its excellent nature."

Not only should mature spiritualists appreciate their exposure to transcendental knowledge but they should also look deeper to ensure that they properly utilize that great opportunity. Someone can go to the best university but that does not necessarily make the person a better student than someone else who went to a general school. It does mean that the person has a greater opportunity because the more advanced school offers better facilities, endowments, and challenges amongst peers. Therefore, the person has a greater likelihood of leaving the school with a higher level of achievement. Nevertheless, if the student does not use the facility properly, he or she will encounter problems. Many of us have distinctly been given a greater opportunity to understand God, the nature of the soul, and how to act. Now we need to look at the way in which we use such opportunities.

We honor such teachers as Moses, Jesus, Mohammed, Buddha, Bahaullah, and so on because we recognize that various prophets come at different times to give a certain type of message. We even honor Sankaracarya, Siva, Ganesh or Durga because we recognize their position as *devas* or demigods. Although we recognize their position as *isvaras* or controllers, we ultimately recognize the position of the *paramesvara* or the Supreme Controller. The Mayavadis and impersonalists fix their goal on the Brahman effulgence or the universal expansion of the Lord. However, we also recognize the existence of the *saktiman* or the energetic source.

Transcendental knowledge actually encompasses Judaism, Christianity, Buddhism, Hinduism, Islam, Taoism, and many other varieties of religions. It gives us distinct information about our ultimate relationship with the Supreme Personality of Godhead and how bona fide religions and teachers are connected. The Vedic scriptures even predict the coming of other *acaryas* in different systems. The *Bhavisya Purana* describes Jesus before he was even born and it mentions Buddha before his presence on this planet. No other scripture goes outside of its own particular theology in such detail. One may then ask, "How can the Vedic scriptures give such predictions?" They can provide these details because sometimes, particular ambassadors repeatedly do similar kinds of work. For example, a citizen of one country might work for the State Department or Foreign Service but then travel to act as the ambassador in other countries to do the same type of work in each particular location. Similarly, some of these great prophets have done the same type of work in other universes; therefore, they act in a similar way when they come to this planet.

The Vaisnava scriptures describe and report on much more than just this planet Earth; they talk about other planets, galaxies, and universes. The entire *Mahabharata* deals with exchanges between extraterrestrials or personalities who have come in from other realms. The Vedic scriptures are very inclusive and encyclopedic. However, practitioners should monitor themselves in order to see how they are applying the knowledge in their own lives. In this way, they can show its elevated status through their good examples. Otherwise, it just becomes fundamentalism and egocentricity in which a person thinks that he or she has the best spouse and disregards everyone else's spouse. We should not think in this mood. We can think that we have a good philosophy but we also honor other prophets and other people's processes. We should happily honor *bhakti* or love of God wherever we find it and avoid sectarianism. Religious fanatics these days often suffer from various mental illnesses. They can so easily put others in distress. Such fanatics can even become terrorists who add to the already growing amount of depression on the planet.

Question: Do you feel that spiritualists suffer from depression and mental illness more than the average person? If so, what causes this phenomenon and how can we help our associates and ourselves overcome such devastating obstacles as we embark on the spiritual path?

Answer: The current statistics show that monks, priests, and nuns have a higher degree of depression than the average populous.[31] Several factors lead to such mental challenges. Obviously, it deals with the fact that they do not fully relate to the normative patterns of society, which results in feelings of isolation. It also stems from the anxieties and feelings of failure that they encounter on the spiritual journey. Some of these negative emotions also have to do with repression of desires. In some cases, it comes from disappointments, expectations, and failures, but in other cases, it has to do with their intense self-lessness, compassion, and longing to fully unite with God.

As we began this section, we stressed the fact that many people come into devotional institutions because of their extreme dissatisfaction with so-called normal life, which more often than not relates to certain types of distress. If such people can be helped, they will grow into very healthy, spiritual entities, but if they do not get the proper help or accept it, they can turn into big disturbances in their institutions and communities and in some cases, even commit suicide. By understanding better how depression can help bring a person into a devotional community, we can also realize the serious results that may occur if expectations are not fulfilled.

Understanding the prevalence of mental illness, which is expected to increase in the coming years at a massive rate, will help us realize that we are not alone. Depression and mental challenges are global problems. As we endeavor to get treatment, we also want to remember that some problems have more of a biological origin than a psychological one. For instance, it has been discovered that even light affects consciousness and a lack of proper lighting can also bring on and accelerate depression. Millions of people have so much self-anger that their mind attacks the body and causes mental as well as physical disease. Some of the other people suffering from depression are products of parents who suffer from alcoholism or drug addiction, which means that they must now deal with fears of abandonment and other mental challenges.

Talk therapy as well as medicinal therapy can help, but at the same time, it can also be very dangerous. One must be selective about their treatments. By understanding the mind better and some of the causes of illness such as mind control and possessions, we will place ourselves in a better position to minimize some of the devastating effects of mental illness. Enthusiasm is most important. One must try to embark upon various projects that enthuse one so that the mind will not have such a tendency to enter into bouts of depression. Sometimes exercise and journaling can help. Prayer is most important along with good *sadhana*. Good association is most essential because our environments will definitely influence us. We should also try to constantly have more gratitude in our lives. This is one of the most powerful ways to expel the virus of depression. Practicing forgiveness is extremely potent. It is also effective to avoid all excessive attachments because most mental illnesses are connected to unhealthy attachments.

Of course, we have the special category of the dark night of the soul. As one deals with the pains of spiritual maturation, the mind cries out due to the bewilderment of the intelligence. Again, we can understand how the mind can be our greatest enemy or greatest friend. When our experiences of depression stem from the dark night of the soul, if we persevere and maintain our faith, the mind will gradually become our greatest friend.

Chapter 6

Addiction and the Process of Recovery

atah kayam imam vidvan
avidya-kama-karmabhih
arabdha iti naivasmin
pratibuddho 'nusajjate

Those who are in full knowledge of
the bodily conception of life, who
know that this body is composed
of nescience, desires and activities
resulting from illusion, do not become
addicted to the body.

Srimad-Bhagavatam 4.20.5

We would like to dedicate this section to the millions, if not billions, of addicts in the world who suffer from addictions to all types of enticements such as alcohol, drugs, food, sex, prestige, and so on. Basically, every living entity has some type of an addiction that controls them in tremendous and unfortunate ways. We want to try to address these people along with ourselves because we will all remain addicts until we actually achieve liberation.

Spiritual Emergency

Materialists are gradually beginning to understand a condition known as a spiritual emergency, which can sometimes develop from the transition of consciousness currently taking place all over the planet. For instance, *kundalini* experiences are among several causes of spiritual crises that can happen during *yoga* practice when the energies move upwards from the spine. Certain people have the ability to develop a higher consciousness or develop entirely different perceptions, and, in many cases, they cannot properly understand or identify these feelings. As a result, they are often placed into mental institutions. Many addicts as well as people in mental institutions are actually undergoing a spiritual crisis that they are not able to deal with or properly balance.

A fine line exists between craziness and spiritual insight because, as a person develops a deep level of spiritual insight, he or she will no longer relate to the environment in the same way. The person will see and think differently, and, in some cases, if he cannot balance those realizations, he might even behave like an insane person. Psychologists and psychiatrists will have to address this phenomenon more and more in the

near future as people who have had contact with extraterrestrials or who have had some stimulating experience simply cannot integrate these experiences into their consciousness. Some
people might even have spiritual experiences that cause them
to lose basic awareness of the body and to feel energized in a
seemingly unnatural way.

Actually, one of the subtle prerequisites for the serious
spiritualist or transcendentalist is the development of a certain
amount of disgust for basic mundane life. As long as a person
thinks of orthodox material life as so grand and wonderful, he
or she will never be able to excel or advance spiritually.

> *bhogaisvarya-prasaktanam*
> *tayapahrta-cetasam*
> *vyavasayatmika buddhih*
> *samadhau na vidhiyate*

> In the minds of those who are too
> attached to sense enjoyment and
> material opulence, and who are
> bewildered by such things, the resolute
> determination for devotional service to
> the Supreme Lord does not take place.
> *Bhagavad-gita* 2.44

Such a person will have tremendous limitations because he
or she will always have the desire to align with the basic objects
of sense gratification and the basic material environments that
stimulate the senses. Often, people who feel disturbed by the
material atmosphere are the best candidates for spiritual life
because they have taken extreme measures to make a consciousness shift or they have made the consciousness shift

without keeping a balance. If these people receive proper guidance, their crises can actually function as a platform from which they can develop a higher understanding or awareness.

Searching after the Ecstasies

Some people underwent various types of spiritual emergencies in the sixties due to their use of psychedelic drugs, which resulted in certain mind-altering experiences that may have stimulated their spiritual pursuit. Although some of these experiences did allow people to connect with their inner faculties, we still do not place any value on artificial stimulants. We are in no way encouraging people to take any type of drug in order to develop their psychic abilities, but we are recognizing that such experiences did act as a catalyst for some people to pursue an alternative or spiritual lifestyle. If we look at the type of person who turns to such stimulants, we will often find someone already pursuing a spiritual lifestyle. In this sense, it is not really the drug itself that makes the change; rather, it is a particular type of consciousness that wants alternatives and searches after the ecstasies.

Actually, if we look at some of the ways in which people try to intoxicate themselves, we will see an insatiable appetite for satisfaction. People are seeking any possible method that will help them make a shift out of their usual mundane consciousness and state of suffering. People will find all types of ways to intoxicate themselves. In some places, people even get high from licking toads. When one licks the toad, it reacts by emanating certain chemicals to protect itself. This chemical affects the person in such a way that it creates an altered state of consciousness. Other people sniff glue and even eat mushrooms to attain an altered state. Of course, such intoxications not only affect the mind but they also affect the body and create a dependency. Alcohol is actually a fermented and rotten drink but people put this substance into their bodies in order to get some stimulation. People also are intoxicating themselves by drinking the fluids used to embalm people. Just consider the whole consciousness that goes along with such an activity.

Ultimately, we all just want to develop a higher consciousness, which is our natural right. We see that practically everyone wants ecstasy or greater experiences in some form. Since we understand that life must involve something greater than just the normal patterns of material life and since we know that we have not yet attained such experiences, we feel a deep sense of dissatisfaction. Some people feel so empty that they will find all types of artificial means to get the quick fix or immediate stimulation. Either they take the drug or they align themselves with some other type of dependency that can temporarily satiate them. For instance, sometimes a person will feel so unloved that they take shelter of food to compensate. They will just eat and eat due to their feeling of emptiness and the food turns into an addiction. Since they want satisfaction and gratification, they will constantly try to acquire that stimulation through the pleasures of the palate and the stomach. If we analyze the different types of addictions, we will see that everyone suffers from some type of dependency. Of course, drugs and alcohol are the most exaggerated forms of addiction, but we should also recognize that we are all motivated by sensual gratifications in general.

The Process of Recovery

Actually, we all subconsciously know that real spiritual

ecstasies are available and waiting for us; however, we just have not yet attained them. In one sense, no one understands the ecstasy or miracle better than the alcoholic because the bottle of alcohol constantly performs a miracle for them. Although it simply incarcerates him or her more, it performs the miracle by changing the person's consciousness and giving some artificial, temporary relief. In recovery, the person has to substitute the miracle of the bottle or drug with the whole process of recovery in order to access the real miracle. The addict must then take shelter of a higher power in order to help maintain that mood.

The Twelve Steps of Alcoholics Anonymous contain many significant and powerful insights about the process of recovery. The process is so extraordinary that if people throughout the world would take advantage of these Twelve Steps, it could trigger a global mind shift. Addiction is quite serious and effective treatment is very profound when properly administered. At different times, people who seem ordinary come into this world with a certain level of empowerment to make a change for millions of people. Some people who have good intentions use this power to provide programs or projects that can help make major shifts on the planet. Alcoholics Anonymous is an empowered program. The program contains many tenets that can allow people to gain a tremendous shift in consciousness and help them accelerate in their understanding of the self.

The Twelve Steps

In the process of recovery, the addict must first past through various stages. Alcoholics Anonymous provides Twelve Steps that we will list and examine in more depth.[32] During the first

stages, the stages of release, the addict mu
that he or she has an addiction. The first
addict understand the depth of their prob
faith in the power of God:

1. We admitted we were powerless over alcohol—that our
   lives had become unmanageable.

2. Came to believe that a Power greater than ourselves could
   restore us to sanity.

3. Made a decision to turn our will and our lives over to the
   care of God *as we understood Him.*

The addict must first recognize their position of utter powerlessness in the presence of the addiction in order to begin
to turn their will over to the care of God. In any process of
transformation and growth including spiritual life, a person
must first understand the nature of their problem and accept
their situation in order to recognize the areas in which they
need to grow. As long as people remain comfortable with the
basic patterns in their daily lives, which basically involve sense
gratification, they will not have a chance to grow sufficiently.
They will remain enslaved by the addiction, which actually
strips them of all freewill. Unless they turn their will over to
God, they will not be able to find relief from the shackles of
the addiction.

The addict must then proceed by focusing on humility and
undergoing an in-depth examination of the self:

4. Made a searching and fearless moral inventory of ourselves.

5. Admitted to God, to ourselves, and to another human being the exact nature of our wrongs.

6. Were entirely ready to have God remove all these defects of character.

7. Humbly asked Him to remove our shortcomings.

8. Made a list of all persons we had harmed, and became willing to make amends to them all.

9. Made direct amends to such people wherever possible, except when to do so would injure them or others.

10. Continued to take personal inventory and when we were wrong promptly admitted it.

Much of the transformation literally happens when alcoholics or addicts meet and discuss their stories. They share among themselves the lowest points in their lives in a way that can lead to healing and growth. As the person develops humility, they also understand that they must stop trying to play God. This idea reoccurs throughout the literatures of Alcoholics Anonymous. The addict must give up the conception that he or she is the Godhead and instead realize that his or her personal strength is not sufficient to overcome the temptations. By accepting that his or her personal strength and resources are not sufficient, the person will begin to recognize the need for a higher power in order to deal with the addiction.

Humility is not an inferiority complex in which we simply lament over our low position that cannot change. Actually, since we have reached such a low point and have completely lost control of our lives, we want to align ourselves with a higher nature and consciously allow that higher nature to control us. This position of humility is very significant in spiritual growth because when a person hits this low point, he or she will then feel extremely eager to do whatever is necessary to rise up from the bottom.

The last steps in this process of recovery involve tolerance and gratitude:

11. Sought through prayer and meditation to improve our conscious contact with God, *as we understood Him*, praying only for knowledge of His will for us and the power to carry that out.

12. Having had a spiritual awakening as the result of these steps, we tried to carry this message to alcoholics, and to practice these principles in all our affairs.

The addict has actually changed his or her external and, most importantly, internal dialogue. As a result, the individual is now very active in sharing and helping others to also undergo a transformation. As the addict develops this quality, he or she learns to tolerate the other members of the group along with other races, religions, and institutions. In this process, addicts also need to stop seeing themselves as victims; rather, they should recognize that all abusers suffer from different types of sicknesses or weaknesses and that everyone needs help due to their particular illness. Therefore, the recovering addict wants to find ways to help other addicts move through their own suffering and incarceration.

The addict should naturally feel gratitude at this point, recognizing the mercy given to them. By accessing gratitude, the person will begin to understand that although they are not really worthy of God's love, grace, and intervention, somehow it is manifesting in their lives. This concept will immediately create a shift in consciousness to such an extent that the person who initially considered themselves to be God's gift to the world and their desires to be foremost will begin to see themselves as the servant of humanity and ultimately of God. They will then feel even more eager to appreciate the mercy that God makes available.

In order to achieve permanent success in this process, we must replace our previous culture, understanding and environment with a more supportive one. Furthermore, we will develop strength just by realizing the gravity of our low position and the need to get some additional support. Of course, this involves turning to the higher power and other supportive people.

Although there is some general knowledge about the treatment of physical addictions, unfortunately, very few therapists in the world know how to treat a spiritual crisis because it goes beyond just the physical addictions. Such people are undergoing a change in their consciousness due to some paranormal experience, which may manifest as erratic or seemingly incoherent behavior. However, some therapists are gradually beginning to understand that the intense craving felt by alcoholics and drug addicts is really a craving for higher love and realizations. Until we have reached the point of liberation, we will remain addicted to various types of sensual stimulations. However, this program is designed to help in some important ways. We must change external behavior while simultaneously going deeper to alter internal awareness and dialogue.

One Day at a Time

I would now like to share a meditation from my book, *The Beggar II*, entitled *One Day at a Time*. This particular meditation compares the recovering alcoholic to the aspiring spiritualist. People often tell the alcoholic that they have a very great and serious problem but the addict should never consider it to be insurmountable. Sometimes if a goal seems inaccessible, we will not even begin the process. However, if we take one step at a time, we will gradually finish one level and move to the next. The process of recovery incorporates this concept of living one day at a time. It encourages us to focus on the immediate achievement without looking at the rest of their week, month, or life as this might simply overwhelm us. By living one day at a time, we can do our best in the present, which will also help us prepare for the next day.

> Dear Lord, is there really any difference between me and the recovering alcoholic? In the beginning, the alcoholic spends years in denial of his addiction, feeling that he is in control and can check his drinking any time he desires.

This happens continuously with alcoholics who initially tell themselves that they will just drink socially or for relaxation. In this way, they deny the fact that they live for the bottle and offer their daily homage to the alcohol.

> But how do I really differ? You see, I am the one who has been in denial—not for

years—but for hundreds of lifetimes. I
have continually taken shelter of my
weak constitution, thinking myself to
be in utter control. But when it comes
to cleansing the garbage that resides in
my mind, I remain at a total loss.

The materialist maintains this type of mindset. Materialists
think that they have everything under their control and neophyte spiritualists also think in this way. However, it is just
a form of denial, which prevents us from addressing deeper
issues. Sometimes we really do not think that we have a problem until we suddenly try to stop some of our improper behavior. Then we realize that we do not have it within our power to
stop. Unfortunately, we cannot make that shift until we realize
the seriousness of the problem. Only when we gain this recognition will we be able to work towards a solution.

My dear Lord, I therefore ask You, is
there really any difference between
me and the recovering alcoholic? The
alcoholic is always thinking about his
past adventures with intoxication. He
often longs to experience that taste
again, but is totally frightened of the
consequences. If he avoids alcoholic
beverages, it is not out of any self-
mastery or discipline, but only out
of cowardice. It is simply because
he is too afraid of the consequences
associated with alcohol.

In other words, we sometimes stop the bad habit temporarily out of fear of the consequences although we have not yet lost the desire. However, gradually that fear will grow into great understanding, appreciation, and avoidance if we follow the process properly.

> Then there is me, the so-called devotee. The seeds of sinfulness are deeply embedded in my consciousness and, even though I don't externally engage in such behaviors, past desires are always there to haunt me. Everyday, I strain to ignore them, but the ghosts of these desires linger lazily in my heart, and never fully go away.

Although we may stop the sinful activities, the sinful desires will still remain for a period of time. But as we develop a deeper understanding, not only will the physical activity permanently cease but the seed of the desire will also stop. At this point, the real transformation takes place.

> *visaya vinivartante*
> *niraharasya dehinah*
> *rasa-varjam raso'py asya*
> *param drstva nivartate*

> The embodied soul may be restricted from sense enjoyment though the taste for sense objects remains. But, ceasing such engagements by

experiencing a higher taste, he is fixed
in consciousness.
Bhagavad-gita 2.59

The recovering alcoholic is completely aware of the seed of the desire. Sometimes addicts will say, "I have been abstinent for twenty years." This means that although they have not taken the alcohol in over twenty years, they still realize what can happen under certain circumstances. They understand that there is always a chance of once again falling prey.

> My dear Lord, I therefore beg You please to tell me—is there really any difference between me and the recovering alcoholic? When former alcohol abusers associate too intimately with one another, they sometimes resume their enslavement to the substance. Collectively and individually, they begin to worship it, meditate on it and think incessantly about various intoxicants. When separated from the bottle even for a moment, they begin to feel as if that separation were lasting for twelve years or more.

In other words, an addiction can be so strong that simply by associating with previous friends and environments, a person can once again revert to old mindsets. An alcoholic with alcoholic parents especially has a greater tendency toward the addiction because it runs in their genes. Due to their family members, they may also carry within the subtle body as well as physical body the tendency to absorb themselves in certain intoxications. For instance, we often see that alcoholism has become such an extensive problem in the Native American culture. Alcoholic parents greatly affect their children because whatever the parent drinks, eats and thinks directly affects the children.

> My addiction was to the cinema. I remember how, not very long ago, I would go to a video store and come home with hours' worth of movies. Just one night without a video would feel to me like an extended jail term. Therefore, I ask you, dear Lord, is there really any difference between me and the recovering alcoholic?
>
> The former drinker tries to reject everything unfavorable to his sobriety, and he eagerly embraces everything that supports it. But all the while he forgets that the great majority of his existence is unfavorable, because a life of continuous fear and struggle to avoid old patterns and old associates is in itself a hellish challenge. I, too, am in this predicament because I must avoid so much of what used to bring me pleasure, now that I realize how incarcerating these activities are.

In one sense, the process of recovery is a type of hell

because the addict must constantly fear situations or relationships that will stimulate the addiction once again.

> What then, O Lord, is the difference
> between me and the recovering
> alcoholic, who goes through his
> day upholding a pretense of normal
> behavior? Although on the outside he
> appears to be coping, in that part of
> him that no one sees, he is internally
> crying out and struggling because his
> addiction has suppressed all other
> desires. Even when he appears to
> have a happy expression, inside he is
> terrified of the mood shifts he knows
> might overcome him if some activity
> plugs him back into his old patterns.

Not all alcoholics have such an obvious problem that makes
them dysfunctional. Many go to work everyday and perform
tremendous activities but they remain fueled and supported by
the alcohol. The alcohol will become such a powerful force
that it even suppresses a person's other desires. We especially
see this happen to the drug addict when the desire for the drug
begins to outweigh the desires for even food, shelter, and sex.

> Dearest Lord, I thus honestly beg
> You please to tell me—is there really
> any difference between me and the
> recovering alcoholic? For former
> drinkers, some days seem to go on
> endlessly, and just waking up the

next morning is almost impossible.
Throughout the day, these ex-addicts
face struggles and challenges at every
step, only to meet similar challenges
the very next day and the next.

Although we have not all directly gone through the process of recovery, we have all had some of these reflections at
difficult times in our lives. At these times, we may go to bed
frustrated and then find it difficult to wake up in the morning
because we do not see any hope. Life becomes very gloomy and
depressive. People also turn to addictions due to tremendous
feelings of gloom and frustration. Whether they have a job, a
family, and money, or they lose all of these possessions, they
simply feel miserable. They end up resorting to a quick death
by suicide or a slow death by taking shelter of a stimulant that
literally destroys the body while altering the consciousness.

As former drinkers look to the future,
sometimes all they have to look
forward to are the adversities of more
and more tests. These recovering
alcoholics travel around and explain to
current addicts how their Higher Power
has allowed them to give up alcohol,
and how others can accomplish this
arduous task. Recovering alcoholics
even boast of being sober for five, ten,
twenty, or even twenty-five years. Still,
no one knows more than they do that
these decades seem like only yesterday,
and that just one sip from a shot glass

can unravel all of their progress. One
sip can make them once again install
a wine or whiskey bottle on the altar
of their consciousness and make this
bottle their worshipable deity.

Even a person on the spiritual path still has the addictions in the background of the consciousness. If the aspiring
spiritualist is not careful, certain moods and situations will
cause him or her to backslide once again and take shelter of
past addictions.

Dear Lord, it was Your great message
carried by Your dedicated messengers
that ultimately cleansed my heart and
pulled me out of the gutter. But how
will I be able to avoid going back into
a gutter mentality that could eventually
degrade me into a gutter existence once
again?
It was then that I heard the voice
of my sweet Lord's servant chuckle
tenderly and non-judgmentally at my
awkward predicament. The voice was
female and full of loving emotion.

Krishna or God has many agents and servants who especially look for those who are trying to make a major shift in
their consciousness. These helpers are accessible.

"My cherished beloved," she said.
"Just like your friend, the recovering

alcoholic, you must learn to take things one day at a time. Temptations are there, but just as you have overcome them so many times in the past to get this far, you must continue warding off these demonic desires to achieve complete mastery of your spiritual technology."

"Now, my child," the melodious voice continued, "maintain and persevere. In fact, enjoy your success rather than lamenting your challenges. You have applied for an advanced degree—of course there will be demanding tests that you will have to pass. However, my precious one, you can rest assured that if you keep sincerely endeavoring to maintain your material sobriety, you will very soon be invited by our Divine Master to thoroughly enjoy spiritual intoxication!

"Unfortunately for you, you are not yet thirsty enough for this position, and so there have been delays in your ascension. But I have confidence that soon you will be very thirsty and eager for this attainment.

"Until that time, just remain firm and fixed in your new lifestyle and go more deeply into your realizations. Do not waste even a moment on extraneous activities. Be very attentive, and avoid all associations that in any way weaken your resolve. And know for sure that we are guiding you. We are all indescribably intoxicated on love of God! But we will be even more blissful when you come and join the eternal party with us and all of your liberated loved ones.

"Always remember that we love you dearly, and that there is no shame in wanting intoxication. Just never settle for the imitation intoxication of the material dimension. Instead, always hanker to partake of the real sweetness of spiritual inebriation by embracing the actual altered state that exists in pure love of God. This can and will come effortlessly, but only when you unhesitatingly love and serve our Supreme Master and dance wildly for His pleasure."

Spiritual Intoxication and Ecstasy

Intoxication is natural and is an ongoing aspect of the soul. The soul is *sac-cid-ananda-vigraha* or eternal, full of knowledge, and full of bliss. The soul in its pure state has overwhelmingly intoxicating experiences, and because we somewhat inwardly know of this sublime intoxication, many take shelter of artificial stimulants in order to try to acquire that experience.

Furthermore, since more and more people feel "blown out" by day-to-day existence and feel unsatisfied, they will want a quick mind shift. As a result, they take shelter of all these different types of artificial stimulants.

As the chaos in the world increases and continues to bombard us on all sides, people will take shelter of many artificial supports and even begin to fall apart. As the demons try to gain control and narcoticize human civilization, they will simply draw in many people who do not know the effects that addiction has on their physical or subtle body and who do not realize how much it interferes with their spiritual evolution. It will even predispose them to the influence of ghosts and other subtle entities. People should not feel comfortable with any type of intoxication, even socially, because it has a tremendous effect on the subtle body and it invites so many negative influences to penetrate.

It is very important for us as aspiring spiritualists to constantly try to help others in their process of spiritual growth rather than just trying to protect or save ourselves. By understanding some of this information, we might find ways to help a person through a spiritual crisis resulting from certain higher energies that they do not know how to process. Recognizing spiritual emergencies can also help us as we begin to acquire higher visions and have contact with higher realms because it will help us understand this seemingly insane mood. If a neophyte has a chance to associate with a higher spiritual being or a carrier of high spiritual energy, some of that energy can spill over onto them. Sometimes the neophyte may even temporarily experience very sublime ecstasies due to the potency of the carrier of such ecstasies. Just as a virus affects people who contact the infected environment, the association of such advanced personalities also will deeply affect the consciousness.

Spiritual entities from very high abodes actually tone themselves down when they enter this particular plane. If they did not tone down their behavior, they would simply seem to be madmen due to their intense, intoxicated love. When certain catalysts stimulate the bliss that they normally experience, their physical body would not be able to contain such spiritual emotions. At times when such people do experience intense spiritual ecstasies, it may externally compare to an epileptic fit because they just cannot contain that energy and consciousness inside the body. Since the physical body cannot cope, the emotions sometimes cause tears to shoot out of the eyes, create tremendous heart palpitations, or even cause them to lose consciousness. These symptoms of deep ecstasy may in fact appear like a state of insanity or mundane intoxication.

We are all crazy in one sense. We are either insanely running after material gratification or we are insanely trying to experience the spiritual ecstasy. We need to ask, "What constitutes normalcy?" Actually, no material culture in the world has any real standard of what constitutes normality. It varies according to time and place; therefore, whatever standards people impose as socially acceptable and "normal" all depend on relative considerations such as time and circumstance. Everyone has some type of insanity but those people who are attached to the material will experience great bewilderment because the temporary, material world can never fully satisfy us. Consequently, people seek the shelter of addictions and stimulations, often with good intentions because they just want the ecstasies and the mind shift. However, even a good intention can lead to degradation rather than acceleration.

Questions and Answers

Question: In your meditation, you explained that alcoholics sometimes feel apprehensive to enter situations in which they might find alcohol. Does that analogy also apply to spiritualists who might feel paranoid about certain gross or subtle material temptations that might not be favorable to devotional service?

Answer: Yes, the neophyte should avoid previous negative associations and environments so that the old patterns will not engulf the person once again. However, after the aspiring spiritualist deeply integrates the spiritual consciousness, he or she can even return to previous environments without being affected. In terms of psychic phenomena, that can also turn into a type of addiction. Sometimes mystical pursuits fascinate people to such an extent that they revolve their entire lives around these mental gymnastics. They spend inordinate amounts of time endeavoring to read auras, engage in channeling, or learn astral projection. This pursuit of subtle energies turns into another form of intoxication and such people will end up trying many different groups and practices, just looking for the bliss. They try various *mantras*, techniques, or workshops with the idea that some formula will solve all their problems. Rather than working on their own consciousness and making a change in their lifestyle, they think that some special amulet, talisman, or *mantra* will solve all their problems.

Question: Recently, I read a magazine article about a woman who ended up addicted to "speed." It suddenly struck me how easily a person can get sucked into an addiction. This single mother tried to work fulltime while raising her child and fulfilling her other duties; however, she just did not have the energy.

In this way, the drug sucked her in by temporarily giving her energy until it destroyed her. I realized how the drugs somewhat fool a person and give a high, but then the person must come down. However, in spiritual life, the high never ends.

Answer: It also shows the danger of just trying to lead a very practical life. We know that the United States government has allowed manufacturers to make certain food products with animal parts and other unhealthy substances without even informing the public. We also understand that certain pharmaceutical drugs are very habit forming. Many people have addictions now due to the allopathic medicine that the doctors gave them. In the 1990's, the tobacco industry was exposed because the manufacturers were actually putting addictive chemicals into the cigarettes.

We will find many situations that can help us recognize the importance of a thoughtful life, free of unhealthy influences and especially addictions. Intoxication is our natural state, but spiritual intoxication rather than material intoxication. To get "the real deal," we must give up the perversion.

Question: I see more and more television programs appearing about UFO abductions and so-called aliens but most seem negative. I do not remember seeing any show on television portraying a positive experience with extraterrestrials, and this seems to create a negative impression.

Answer: Just a few years ago, I recorded a program for National Television with the host of a show in Ghana on UFOs and extraterrestrials at the Institute for Applied Spiritual Technology. We discussed the phenomena of pyramids, UFOs, and extraterrestrials in relation to *bhakti* or devotional service to God. I have given lectures to psychiatrists at the University of Michigan and to hundreds of psychiatrists in Siberia on these topics. Sometime earlier, I met a lady who works with the American Psychological Association and had written a book about abductions, which surprised me.[33] At first, it amazed me that these topics were being discussed in such orthodox circles. Actually, such topics are gradually being discussed in many circles because they can no longer be contained. There are many reasons to believe that in the coming years, not only will people discuss these issues more but certain world changes will also help people understand more about the connection that beings on this planet have with some of the other realms.

At this particular time, increasing activity is taking place among entities from the lower realms and the higher realms. Many souls are acting as mediums and many ancient prophets have even come back again. There are prophets who have been away for many millennia and have come back at this particular time because the planet is going through major shifts. Almost every week in America, we see or hear about unusual phenomena. However, anything powerful has both polarities, which means that some people's experiences are not so auspicious. The idea of abduction itself is not so wonderful because it implies that someone takes another person by force without the element of love. At the same time, we are at a period in which sin is more dominant than piety. If we look at how the average people live their lives, we will see a predomination of sin.

Some of the people involved in the sinful plan actually want to create confusion in people's minds about these topics. However, the earth has always been a planet that higher personalities have cared for; therefore, some of the caretakers who have a direct responsibility are returning to help in the consciousness-raising campaign. We will see many miracles happening in the coming years. Even some of you, beloved, have always felt that you have a mission and that you do not quite fit into the normal scheme of material life. Those types of sentiments are not just conceptual. In the coming years, as the environment accelerates, people will become much more sensitive. Even if we just look at the last five years, we will recognize an increasing emphasis on channeling and mediums, which indicates an increase in the contact between different dimensions. Even ten years ago, some of the programs on UFOs and other related topics would never have even appeared on television. However, if you go to almost any major bookstore now, you will find many books on these sorts of topics. As a matter of fact, they are some of the most popular books in the United States.

About twenty years ago, I gave a radio program and I remember when I mentioned UFOs, the mood of the audience shifted dramatically. People would call in and say, "Swami, I really liked your program but that UFO stuff is hard to accept." People responded the same way in one call after another. However, we can speak more openly on this topic now, even in our tape ministry. During the last three years, our biggest selling tapes addressed topics related to unconditional love and extraterrestrials. During the last six years, in one of our newer *Spiritual Warrior* books, we address this topic in one of the chapters due to the increasing interest in so many circles. Actually, this increasing exposure to psychic phenomena is preparing people to become more aware of their spiritual existence as well as more aware of the connection between the earth planet and other existences. It will also help people understand that there is a much grander plan to life than just the normal day-to-day problems.

Real changes happen in the world in times of crisis and

emergencies. Usually, everyone remains so captured by the daily activities that it takes tremendous situations to really force them to change. Otherwise, they simply focus on paying the rent or mortgage, going to work, making money for someone else, coming home, finding food, falling asleep, and then preparing for the same cycle the next day. This lifestyle leaves little time to even think or really pursue much more than this typical cycle. This cycle causes many people to pursue mundane intoxications of all kinds, which will interfere with the ability to become spiritually intoxicated with *prema*, divine love.

Chapter 7

Laughter Good for the Body and Soul

brahma-bhutah prasannatma
na socati na kanksati
samah sarvesu bhutesu
mad-bhaktim labhate param

One who is thus transcendentally situated at once realizes the Supreme Brahman and becomes fully joyful. He never laments or desires to have anything. He is equally disposed toward every living entity. In that state he attains pure devotional service unto Me.

Bhagavad-gita 18.54

Laughter as an Antidote

Worry, fear, anger, grief, and depression are distinct enemies that are very expert in attacking our minds. They are constantly waiting for an opportunity to intrude into our consciousness, but they cannot enter unless we invite them in. They need a host. If by some mistake, accident, or lack of attentiveness we let them in, we must quickly escort them out, as we would an unwanted guest. Laughter is one of the powerful ways that we get rid of such a guest. These enemies do not want to be associated with a cheerful person, which means that if they have already entered, they will immediately feel unwelcome. If they find that laughter is being hosted, they will go elsewhere instead of trying to remain.

Most modern researchers on this subject accept that all humans have a natural potential to develop a sense of humor. In studies conducted on infant and child development, findings indicate that it is a very innate and necessary activity, which naturally manifests even at this young age.[34] Most healthy adults laugh up to twenty times a day, and children up to two hundred. We all enjoy it and recognize it. Philosophers such as Plato, Aristotle, Hume, and Kant have even written about laughter. It binds those who are sharing a joke by relaxing them and often connecting them on a deep level. It often builds up rapidly, and is a cue for others to join in. In its own way, it seeks out fellowship and community.

Laughter and humor can foster a hopeful and positive attitude. We are less likely to succumb to feelings of anxiety, fear, anger, depression, and grief if we are able to laugh at what troubles us. Laughter provides an opportunity for the release of uncountable unhealthy emotions, which will create destructive biochemical changes to the body and mind if we

hold them within. Through laughter, we can
our best antidotes to these enemies of the mind
who are already wounded by these enemies hav
to laugh. Some of you who are wounded will nave a difficult
time remembering the last time you had a tumultuous laugh. It
is important that you protect and build up your mind and body
with healthy laughter. After all, it's painless, it's accessible, and
it's free.

Accelerate the Joy

Not only is laughter one of the expressions of spiritual
ecstasy, but it is also good for the body and soul. Sometimes
we take ourselves far too seriously along with our faults,
successes, and current challenges. Initially, this may sound
strange because in devotional service we are to be focused and
determined in order to rise above the modes of material nature.
We do realize that no one can get out of this material world if
they have too much attachment to the activities of *martya-loka*
or the material world of death. We also realize that we must
control the mind and conquer over the senses; however, while
engaging in all the strict rules and regulations, we must simultaneously accelerate the joy. The process ultimately culminates
in an eternal festival and romance. The goal is an eternal adventure in which the devotees of the Lord are in a constant state of
intoxication and happiness as they appreciate God's love. They
constantly find ways to invoke more love, sometimes through
hilarious exchanges.

Sometimes spiritualists are so grave, dry, and impersonal
that they even scare people away. Regardless of the spiritual
tradition or religion, some practitioners develop such a mood

of renunciation and austerity that their hearts harden. Many of the great *acaryas* and religious teachers were very austere, but they were not trying to torture themselves. We realize that they eagerly wanted to embrace the higher pleasures; therefore, their renunciation involved removing unnecessary obstacles so that they could go deeper. When we look at the activities that constantly unfold in the spiritual paradigm, we will see that the unalloyed devotees are full of joy, even in the most difficult and trying situations. They always experience eternal joy since they understand that everything ultimately rests on God:

> *mattah parataram nanyat*
> *kincid asti dhananjaya*
> *mayi sarvam idam protam*
> *sutre mani-gana iva*

> O conqueror of wealth, there is no truth
> superior to Me. Everything rests upon
> Me, as pearls are strung on a thread.
> *Bhagavad-gita* 7.7

Laughter as a Therapy

In the ancient cultures and especially in monarchical arrangements, the king would often have a jester. The jesters endeavored to incite laughter in the royal court and give wisdom through humor. They sought to create a greater sense of community by acting as a catalyst for laughter. Modern therapists, sociologists, physiologists, and biologists are also gradually beginning to understand the unique and powerful results of laughter. Many different therapies, which doctors or psychologists use to treat depression and even physical sickness, involve laughter. It works because we understand that all emotions and sentiments have a deeper connection with the soul. Such emotions relate to the ecstasy that arises from engagement in the loving service of the Lord. They develop from the powerful reciprocation a living entity experiences in his or her relationship with the Supreme Personality of Godhead. In one sense, we can ultimately associate real laughter with spiritual activities. Comedians are popular because they help people get out of their ordinary mindsets. However, this type of humor is simply a dim reflection of the actual exchange of ecstasy and laughter between the Lord and the devotees.

In the material world, comedians might radiate just a tiny reflection of this ultimate position of joy in the spiritual world. Such comedians recognize the need to help stimulate the society and sometimes look at serious situations from a lighter perspective. They might attack the President or some very important person in order to show the ridiculous side. They might show the insignificance of a person who thinks of himself or herself as very important. It shows the insignificance of the person's words and actions. In this way, comedians help remind us that we are not as important as we think. Sometimes we think that life will not go on if we do not carry out specific duties or functions, but such egocentric thinking may not be the most beneficial.

At times, when we do not make the mark, we should not put so much weight on ourselves by realizing that it never solely just relates to us. We are eternally parts and parcels of the Supreme Personality of Godhead who have an eternal service that nobody can take away from us. If we lose our jobs or a very valuable possession, we can try to laugh, realizing that we really lost nothing because we never owned the job or the object. And nobody can ever take away that which we really do own. We can see our feeling of bereavement as a joke in one sense because all of our possessions are relative and superficial compared to our eternal property. If we change our perspective, we do not have to feel disturbed by our lack of a job or by the seemingly unfortunate situations that sometimes happen in the material energy. We can see it as the Lord's way to remind us of our eternal identity, which is greater than all of these temporary distractions. The Lord tries to remind us so we will not feel too comfortable trying to enjoy the relative pleasures. He wants us to come forward and enjoy the eternal mysteries and pleasures with Him.

Physical and Mental Benefits of Laughter

Just as stress has been shown to create unhealthy physiological changes, laughter creates the opposite effects. It appears to be the perfect antidote for stress. It has been proven that laughter relaxes the muscles in the body and oxygenates the blood. It benefits the cardiovascular system; exercises the heart; enhances circulation and increases the oxygen transport; improves the distribution of nutritional elements within the system; and increases immune responsivity. Laughter also decreases the perception of pain, thus acting as a natural painkiller.[35]

Through laughter, patients in hospitals are able to forget about their pains, diseases, and distress. Laughter gives hope and a feeling of well-being. In this way, we can access more of our soul's quality. When we do not feel grateful and instead accept the anxiety stemming from our problems, the body emits adrenaline into the system, which constricts the arteries, produces high blood pressure, and weakens the immune system. It can cause all types of diseases and even death.

We just have to remind ourselves that these bodies are machines that function as such. Certain activities and mindsets will help the machine function very powerfully and some will weaken the machine. Although we want to emphasize the fact that the body or machine that we temporarily possess is not eternally ours, we still need to take care of it since we must use it every day. We do not want to deny its importance or go to the other extreme by focusing all of our attention on it; rather, we want to use it wisely while we have the chance. Some people identify with all of the issues that happen to them and to the society in general, which does not lead to the most positive results.

The United Nations estimates that approximately 180 million people around the world over 15 years of age were consuming drugs by the end of the twentieth century.[36] For most people, it stems from stress and anxiety. They take shelter of such intoxicants to relieve the stress. Furthermore, estimates suggest that 5.5 million people have a pathological gambling problem and 15 million people are at risk.[37] It all stems from distress that people feel because they want thrill and excitement. They want the quick economic fix. They find themselves enslaved since they do not have the ability to step back from their situation and laugh at the challenges. People identify with the temporary without recognizing God's love or the essence. They do not have a sense of laughter that will help them think, "I am not my body anyway. I have allowed the illusion to maintain these false conceptions and failed to acknowledge the Lord's arrangements in my life." We can see the intensity of people's dissatisfaction simply by observing these statistics.

Laugh at the Illusion

Some people, especially these days, definitely do not laugh because they have a whole host of problems. Of course, whether we are poor, wealthy, sick, or healthy, we all have a host of problems and we actually increase our problems because we do not have a sense of detachment. If we do not access a sense of laughter, instead of eradicating the problem, we may actually intensify and amplify the issue. For this reason, excessive lamentation is not healthy. Obviously, we need to grieve at times so that we do not fall into a state of denial but we have to face issues and then release them. We can release the issues by acknowledging God's constant presence and by realizing that we are not the ultimate controllers. We can try to maintain this reflection in spite of any external challenges by remembering that our supreme Father loves us more than anyone and He has that love for us at all times. We have the ultimate security because, in spite of whatever happens to our body and our material facilities, we realize that God's love and protection for our soul always remains. Sometimes we focus too much on our bodies, and this entangles us in more distress, but if we can remember that we are not our bodies, we will feel relief.

We can use this reflection to help us through many setbacks. If we lose our job, at the end of the day we can feel glad that we are not our job. We are not our house, car, or any of the other material amenities that we use everyday. Sometimes we can laugh at ourselves when we forget this basic fact and begin to think of these temporary objects as essential to our actual existence. We can laugh at the intensity with which we embrace the illusion and at the strength of the illusion. From time to time, we can gratefully remind ourselves that we are separate from such temporary situations. We can thank the Lord because His love is greater than His law and His love is also manifesting when He sends us material obstacles that will ultimately help us return to His abode.

Laughter Minimizes the Seemingly Monumental Problems

We sometimes spend so much time focusing on the body in an endeavor to make it look nicer but in spite of all the modern technologies such as plastic surgery, one day the body will age. We will look at ourselves in the mirror and wonder what happened to the body that used to be so youthful and attractive. The hair will turn gray and the body will expand in places that we do not feel comfortable with. Our memory will decrease and many wrinkles will set in.

At this stage, many people feel overwhelmed with anxiety and lose a sense of self-esteem. However, the spiritualist can laugh at the situation, realizing that the machine will continue to make even more shifts over the course of time. One day we will even have to abandon the machine, but we can feel excited, knowing that we have an identity separate from the machine. We have had many other machines, and if we are not careful, we may even have to accept a few more bodies. Nevertheless, we are not our bodies or our disturbed minds that are experiencing anxiety, anger, fear, grief, and depression. With this thought in mind, we can look at the most difficult times in our lives and view them as experiences. We can also look at the most wonderful times in our past and recognize them as another flickering aspect of the body.

When we have a failure or make a mistake, we need to

understand the difference between temporarily failing and viewing ourselves as failures. We do not have to take a mistake or a failure so seriously. Actually, the problem escalates when we allow the failure to encompass our whole existence. The failure will threaten our well-being when we begin to accept that setback as our identity. However, we should laugh at that thought because how can entities who eternally love and associate with the Supreme Lord be failures? If we can acknowledge our permanent identity as healthy, knowledgeable, blissful, and full of love, we can laugh at the insignificant moments in our existence in which we forget that reality. We might have failed in some area but we are not failures.

Even Thomas Edison made over one 1,000 mistakes in his attempt to invent the light bulb, but each time he saw it as a chance to come closer to the conclusion. Each time he saw it as an opportunity to try a new experiment after ruling out the last possibility. Especially when we endeavor to increase our faith and direct our consciousness to the spiritual realm, we can always step back from time to time and just feel gratitude and happiness as we acknowledge the Lord's constant presence.

Sometimes we struggle economically but we can also laugh at that temporary circumstance because in other lifetimes, we have had exorbitant wealth. Even in this lifetime, we have periods in which we have more security. If we can mentally remove ourselves from the immediate anxiety, we will discover that whether we have wealth or not, we have not found happiness in this material world. We realize that we will not feel any deep sense of satisfaction as long as we remain separate from God. Some people who have fame, distinction, and adoration actually receive a type of blessing because in spite of all of their opulences, they still feel miserable. They have received a blessing in disguise because they can now pursue something

beyond material security and opulence. If
completely satisfied them, they would be lo:
struggle for survival and would not have ar
for a higher level of fulfillment outside of tl

See the Challenge as an Opportunity

This just shows the extraordinary nature of the Lord's plan
because we will inevitably feel some lack in any seemingly
material auspicious or inauspicious situation. We can try to
recognize all of our circumstances as Krishna's mercy, which
we can use to reflect on the essence. We want to be a part of the
eternal *lila* or pastimes of the Lord although we have temporarily separated ourselves from that eternal reality. The living
entities in this material world are staging a drama in which they
hide from the Lord. We might compare this to a game of hide-
and-seek in which the children hide from the parents although
the parents know the hiding spot. They simply pretend to look
for the child in order to increase the excitement of the game.

We are actually temporarily hiding from the Supreme
Personality of Godhead and He is watching to see how long
we intend to continue with our pretence. We have absorbed
ourselves in this false game, thinking of ourselves as unloved,
which simply leads us to complain about our unhappiness and
lack of fulfillment. We are basically hiding from our real identity and we can play this game for as long as we desire. But
even while we play this game, we can feel excited, knowing
that someday we will find relief from this drama. The Supreme
Personality of Godhead does not just let us remain in such a
situation without arranging for our exit. However, while struggling through the challenge, it might seem that He has taken

His love away from us. This results from our illusions and temporary thoughts and actions. We can have a very big laugh here—Ha-ha Ha-ha Ha-ha—as we realize how real this existence of virtual reality appears to be and how we so often allow ourselves to fully accept the illusions.

Biographical Reflections

We have all found ourselves in intense situations that seemed extremely serious, but sometimes when we took a step back, we found ourselves breaking out in laughter. If we can just see the humor from time to time, it gives a sense of relief because of its connection with an actual *rasa* or mellow associated with Krishna. This connection can in some way help remind us to come back home to the spiritual realm. We want to remember not to take ourselves too seriously by identifying with material situations as the all in all. By identifying with temporary realities, we will miss the chance to reconnect with our real identity and our real engagements.

While reflecting on laughter from many of these different perspectives, I also took a few minutes to look at the biographical perspective in my own life. My mother, who has left her body, would sometimes remind me of an experience from my childhood that involved the false perception of thinking myself to be the center of attraction as well as the center of my insecurities. She was quite a spiritual lady and had an interesting way of guiding all of her children. Sometimes in the past when she would see me on television, see pictures of me meeting presidents and diplomats of countries, or receive reports from my disciples about my work in various countries, she would bring up this specific memory from my past.

She told me that she once found me in a state of deep reflection in the backyard although I was only four years old. Sometimes children may shock us because they can be quite intense at times. They are not really children but actually adults in small bodies. This means that they may also carry some amazing phobias with them. Basically, I had a phobia of ants, spiders, and rats just to name a few. These fears started all the way back at four years old.

After looking at some ants in the backyard, I looked up at my mother and said, "I know what they are doing. They are discussing and planning to see which one of them will bite me first." Although I was just four years old, I thought everything revolved around me. I had such a fear of these little ants that I actually thought they were having a conference and discussing their plan to bite me. My mother would sometimes remind me of my insignificance by saying, "You are not so important, wonderful, or secure. You are the person who always thinks that someone is trying to bother or bite you." Imagine a little old lady telling her so-called famous, renounced, puffed-up son this statement. Come on, let's laugh together on this one!

I had another experience while attending a very exclusive prep school, which I entered after finishing a ghetto school in Cleveland. This prep school catered to very wealthy people so I was like an experiment for them. I was the only African-American and the first to graduate from the school. While attending, I joined the track team and also wrestled. The superintendent of this school had this theory that African-Americans have special legs that enable them to run better. Maybe he read some report but somehow or other he came to this conclusion. He seemed to think, "Now that we have this black boy on the team, we will see some great excellence."

At some point, our team prepared to compete in a very

important event and they considered me the big anchor on the field. Everyone was watching me as we prepared to run this long, two-mile race. However, I started off improperly by just sprinting as fast as possible—an unwise technique for a long race. A runner should balance him or herself in order to keep running for the duration of the race. Regardless, I started off so fast, trying to impress everyone. For about four or five minutes I was beating everyone, but then all my high energy just left and I could not even maintain my normal ability that I would have had if I had begun slowly. Consequently, I came in last—we lost. What a laugh!

A similar experience happened to me in a wrestling match but now I can look back and laugh, realizing how much I played into the idea of being important. I was identifying with my body and with a mythology while trying to be wonderful. However, the Lord in His own way helped me to realize that I must not over-identify with any type of mundane designation. Of course, now I can look back and laugh, but while undergoing the event, the humiliation was devastating. I had to walk off the field, knowing that I had caused the whole team to lose by not coming up to everyone's expectations. At times, we might have to face a seemingly negative situation, which might seem overwhelming and painful, but later we can look back and laugh. We can realize that such painful experiences only make up a small part of our existence that we are literally passing through. **We are not these experiences.**

During another period in my life spent at the prestigious Princeton University in the United States of America, I went through a phase in which I tried to run away from God. However, I can see how He so expertly prevents us from running too far away. During that time, I was doing all kinds of deviant things and even at one point taking intoxication. I would often cause my roommates to laugh because every time I would get intoxicated, I would start preaching or talking about God. I would become extremely philosophical. During any party or gathering, my friends would practically wait and watch for that moment when I would begin to preach. They would just smile, knowing that it would come any time soon. And when it did, they would break out in laughter and then listen. Although I was trying to run away from the Lord, now I can look back and laugh, realizing that He was still showering His kindness on me. The Lord was trying to hold onto me by making arrangements that would impel me to think more about spiritual activities instead of the normal material activities.

We can all look at different times in our lives in which we took ourselves too seriously. For this reason, I shared these few stories from my own life, which show the relativity of such experiences. It can also help us see how God always remains with us in spite of the seemingly negative circumstances.

The Process of Surrender

The twelfth chapter of the *Bhagavad-gita* shows how the Lord accommodates us in many ways. First He tells us to always think of Him in spite of any external situation. However, if we find it difficult to always think of God, we can engage in the process of *sadhana-bhakti*, which involves devotional rituals and activities, so that we engage our mind and senses in the service of the Lord. These devotional practices will help us to identify less with the material paradigm and gradually come to the point of always thinking of the Supreme Personality of Godhead. It is not that the rules and regulations alone are essential but we need them in our own growth because we are not always thinking of God. We engage in all of the ninefold activities in order to increase our ability to always think of Krishna. This is the position of the *nitya-siddhas* or eternally pure devotees. Their connection with the spiritual paradigm goes far beyond a mere reflection; rather, they have genuinely absorbed themselves in the reality and do not feel any of the illusion of separation.

We need to remind ourselves again and again that genuine spiritual life involves that deep level of absorption. God is *atmarama* or self-satisfied which means that He does not need anything from us, but He wants us to be whole again by fully absorbing ourselves in transcendence. This is *saranagati* or surrender. Surrender really means that interferences no longer block our absorption in the reality. As we engage in the spiritual practices, we can remind ourselves that all of the material challenges and obstacles we encounter are a part of the process for breaking out of the *maha-tattva* or the illusions and the material prison. Our existence in these material bodies might even feel like a nightmare at times, but just as we feel relief when we wake up from a nightmare at night, we will feel great relief when we wake up from this grand illusory nightmare. Sometimes we can even laugh about our complete absorption in the nightmare and at the extent that we have accepted it as a reality. Join me with a big laugh for we have allowed ourselves to be tricked so deeply. Some of the greatest laughter comes when someone misses the obvious or is serious in a ridiculous situation. We are so outrageous. Ha-ha Ha-ha Ha-ha!

Utsaha or enthusiasm is so essential to devotional service because enthusiasm somehow keeps us moving. If we lose it, we will start identifying with this realm of duality. Enthusiasm comes from a Greek word referring to God and also within. This can help us understand that enthusiasm really has to do

with our internal life, which we cannot fake
others but we cannot fake it to ourselves. If
our constant acceptance of the temporary, v
to feel enthusiastic. We will function on a
nally we will feel depressed or disturbed. We will experience
setbacks due to our mental culture. However, when we accept
more of God's mercy on us and really have faith in its presence
in our lives, we will have great and dynamic internal strength.
When we experience all kinds of dangers that constantly plague
us everyday in the world, we have to recognize the reality of
these problems but still acknowledge its temporary nature in
terms of the total scheme of reality. It does mean looking at
our whole existence differently without taking our external
situations as the total reality. Then we can even laugh at our
extensive submersion in the drama and begin to recognize that
we are just actors in this grand play.

Insights from the Scriptures

The *Srimad-Bhagavatam* describes how we can see the
difficulties that we experience on the devotional path as an
exchange of *bhava* or love and ecstasy with the Lord. The commentary to *Srimad-Bhagavatam* 1.9.19 states, "Tribulations
imposed upon the devotees by the Lord constitute another
exchange of transcendental *bhava* between the Lord and the
devotees. The Lord says 'I put My devotee into difficulty, and
thus the devotee becomes more purified in exchanging transcendental *bhava* with Me.' Placing the devotee into material
troubles necessitates delivering him from the illusory material
relations." The Lord reveals that He often personally puts His
devotees into difficulty because it can assist them in accessing

more spiritual depth and prevent them from aligning entirely with the external realm. As they connect more with the internal realities, it becomes a part of the adventure and the mystery of spirituality. It becomes a part of the animated association and joy that eternally unfolds in the spiritual world. In this way, the challenge turns into an exchange of *bhava* between the Lord and His devotees.

As transcendentalists, we do not pray to have obstacles removed but we do pray for the ability to see God's presence in all of these situations. We want to pray in the mood of Queen Kunti in the *Srimad-Bhagavatam* who prayed for more challenges as long as they helped her to remember the Supreme Lord again and again. Transcendence is not an ordinary affair because it ultimately means that we come to a point in which we do not allow any obstacle to check the radiant love emanating from the Lord or the love that we offer back to Him. All of our activities on the path of self-realization really should help us recognize the illusory nature of the world of duality. Although it temporarily exists, it is not the entirety of the reality. It is part of the adventure of meeting the parents again after the child has been playing hide-and-go-seek. They experience the adventure of separation and then the ecstasy of meeting together as one family.

According to Vaisnava philosophy, the personality, Madhumangala, for instance, compares to a transcendental jester in the court who finds ways to create laughter and remind others of the joy through his humorous activities. If we look closer at some of Madhumangala's activities, his pranks and jokes would overwhelm us. However, he creates these humorous pastimes for the pleasure of Krishna and the *gopas* who enjoy his jokes. Even Krishna plays pranks on Radharani and Radharani plays pranks on Krishna. Sometimes the *gopis* in

different camps play pranks on each other. Krishna consciousness ultimately involves these simple but loving exchanges and
we want to prepare ourselves to have the innocence of small
children engaged in play. They do not have to worry about
bills, health, or sex anxiety. Children just have an innocence
that is actually the nature of the soul.

The passages from the Vedic scriptures can shed more light
on this topic, especially the *Nectar of Devotion*:

> In the fourth division of *Bhakti-
> rasamrta-sindhu*, Srila Rupa Gosvami
> has described seven kinds of indirect
> ecstasies of devotional service,
> known as laughing, astonishment,
> chivalry, compassion, anger, dread
> and ghastliness. In this portion, Srila
> Rupa Gosvami further describes
> these ecstasies of devotional feelings,
> some being compatible and others
> incompatible with one another. When
> one kind of ecstatic devotional service
> overlaps with another in a conflicting
> way, this state of affairs is called
> *rasabhasa*, or a perverted presentation
> of mellows. Expert learned scholars say
> that laughing is generally found among
> youngsters or in the combination of old
> persons and young children.

We see this more actively when we watch children play
because they have a unique type of innocence. They display
a simple attitude because they do not have the same anxieties

that we have. For this reason, some scriptures emphasize that we have to become like children in order to become born again. This indicates the importance of humility and submissiveness, which are childlike qualities. Then we see this description of laughter between children and elders in the *Nectar of Devotion* because as we age, we also begin to revert to childlike innocence once again. There is a very sweet exchange between the young and the old as they experience that innocence. Sometimes when people are elderly and retired, they can again access that innocence after renouncing certain entanglements. Of course, the Vedic scriptures recommend that we are to elevate ourselves to the ultimate level of renunciation as we prepare ourselves to make our transition.

The *Nectar of Devotion* continues to elaborate on these pastimes of laughing ecstasy:

> This ecstatic loving laughing is sometimes also found in persons who are very grave by nature. Once an old mendicant approached the door of mother Yasoda's house, and Krishna told Yasoda, "My dear mother, I don't wish to go near this skinny villain. If I go there, he might put Me within his begging bag and take Me away from you!" In this way, the wonderful child, Krishna, began to look at His mother, while the mendicant, who was standing in the door, tried to hide his smiling face, although he could not do so. He immediately expressed his smiling. In this instance, Krishna Himself is the object of laughing affairs.

Once one of Krishna's friends informed Him, "My dear Krishna, if You will open Your mouth, then I shall give You one nice sugar candy mixed with yogurt." Krishna immediately opened His mouth, but instead of giving Him sugar candy with yogurt, the friend dropped a flower in His mouth. After tasting this flower, Krishna turned His mouth in a disfigured way, and upon seeing this all His friends standing there began to laugh very loudly.

Once a palmist came to the house of Nanda Maharaja, and Nanda Maharaja asked him, "My dear sage, will you kindly check the hand of my child, Krishna? Tell me how many years He will live and whether He will become the master of thousands of cows." Upon hearing this, the palmist began to smile, and Nanda Maharaja asked him, "My dear sir, why are you laughing, and why are you covering your face?"

The palmist found this small question hilarious in comparison to Krishna's real potency and greatness. He could understand Krishna's awesomeness by recognizing His supreme dominion not only over thousands of cows but over the entire creation.

In such a laughing ecstasy of love, Krishna or matters pertaining to Krishna are the cause of the laughter. In

such laughing devotional service, there
are symptoms of jubilation, laziness,
concealed feelings and similar other
seemingly disturbing elements.

According to Srila Rupa Gosvami's
calculation, laughter in ecstatic love
can be broken down into six divisions.
These divisions, according to different
degrees of smiling, are called in
the Sanskrit language *smita*, *hasita*,
vihasita, *avahasita* and *atihasita*.
These six classes of smiling can be
classified as major and minor. The
major division includes *smita*, *hasita*
and *vihasita* smiling, and the minor
division includes *avahasita*, *apahasita*
and *atihasita* smiling.

When one is smiling but his teeth
are not visible, one can distinctly mark
a definite change in the eyes and in the
cheeks. This is called *smita* smiling.
Once when Krishna was stealing
yogurt, Jarati, the headmistress of
the house, could detect His activities,
and she was therefore coming very
hurriedly to catch Him. At that time,
Krishna became very much afraid of
Jarati and went to His elder brother,
Baladeva. He said, "My dear brother, I
have stolen yogurt! Just see—Jarati is
coming hurriedly to catch Me!" When
Krishna was thus seeking the shelter of

Baladeva because He was being chased by Jarati, all the great sages in the heavenly planets began to smile. This smiling is called *smita* smiling.

Smiling in which the teeth are slightly visible is called *hasita* smiling. One day Abhimanyu, the so-called husband of Radharani, was returning home, and at that time he could not see that Krishna was there in his house. Krishna immediately changed His dress to look exactly like Abhimanyu and approached Abhimanyu's mother, Jatila, addressing her thus: "My dear mother, I am your real son Abhimanyu, but just see—Krishna, dressed up like me, is coming before you!" Jatila, the mother of Abhimanyu, immediately believed that Krishna was her own son and thus became very angry at her real son who was coming home. She began to drive away her real son, who was crying, "Mother! Mother! What are you doing?" Seeing this incident, all the girl friends of Radharani, who were present there, began to smile, and a portion of their teeth was visible. This is an instance of *hasita* smiling.

When the teeth are distinctly visible in a smile, that is called *vihasita*. One day when Krishna was engaged in stealing butter and yogurt in the house of Jatila, He assured His friends, "My dear friends, I know that this old lady is now sleeping very profoundly, because she is breathing very deeply. Let us silently steal butter and yogurt without making any disturbance." But the old lady, Jatila, was not sleeping; so she could not contain her smiling, and her teeth immediately became distinctly visible. This is an instance of *vihasita* smiling.

In a state of smiling when the nose becomes puffed and the eyes squint, the smiling is called *avahasita*. Once, early in the morning when Krishna returned home after performing His *rasa* dance, mother Yasoda looked upon Krishna's face and addressed Him thus: "My dear son, why do Your eyes look like they have been smeared with some oxides? Have You dressed Yourself with the blue garments of Baladeva?" When mother Yasoda was addressing Krishna in that way, a girl friend who was nearby began to smile with a puffed nose and squinting eyes. This is an instance of *avahasita* smiling. The *gopi* knew that Krishna had been enjoying the *rasa* dance and that mother Yasoda could not detect her son's activities or understand how He had become covered with the *gopis'* makeup. Her smiling was in the *avahasita* feature.

When a smiling person claps his hands and leaps in the air, the smiling expression changes into *atihasita*, or overwhelming laughter. An example of *atihasita* was manifested in the following incident. Krishna once addressed Jarati thus: "My dear good woman, the skin of your face is now slackened, and so your face exactly resembles a monkey's. As such, the King of the monkeys, Balimukha, has selected you as his worthy wife." While Krishna was teasing Jarati in this way, she replied that she was certainly aware of the fact that the King of the monkeys was trying to marry her, but she had already taken shelter of Krishna, the killer of many powerful demons, and therefore she had already decided to marry Krishna instead of the King of the monkeys. On hearing this sarcastic reply by the talkative Jarati, all the cowherd girls present there began to laugh very loudly and clap their hands. This laughter, accompanied by the clapping of hands, is called *atihasita*.

Sometimes there are indirect sarcastic remarks which also create *atihasita* circumstances. An example of one such remark is a statement which was made by one of the cowherd girls to

Kutila, the daughter of Jatila and sister of Abhimanyu, the so-called husband of Radharani. Indirectly Kutila was insulted by the following statement: "My dear Kutila, daughter of Jatila, your breasts are as long as string beans—simply dry and long. Your nose is so gorgeous that it defies the beauty of the noses of frogs. And your eyes are more beautiful than the eyes of dogs. Your lips defy the flaming cinders of fire, and your abdomen is as beautiful as a big drum. Therefore, my dear beautiful Kutila, you are the most beautiful of all the cowherd girls of Vrndavana, and because of your extraordinary beauty, I think you must be beyond the attraction of the sweet blowing of Krishna's flute!"[38]

From these few descriptions of laughing ecstasy in the Vaisnava literatures, we can see how laughter and dance are an integral part of the spiritual experience. The eternal residents do not take themselves so seriously. They are always involved in loving sport and romance, centering everything upon the Supreme Personality of Godhead. This is their eternal identity. It is not that one intensely engages in devotional service just to return to a boring environment or should engage in austerities, successes, and failures in a way that one misses the joy of spiritual life.

Find the Humor in Daily Life

We must now remind ourselves not to forget to laugh. If we fail, we understand that we do not become that failure. We simply "goofed" in that situation. If we have some disappointment, loss, difficulty, or anxiety, we must address the problem while maintaining a sense of detachment. We might experience the six enemies of the mind but we are not these enemies. They attack us and even temporarily overtake us but we still have a separate identity. We want to be able to recognize God's mercy in the midst of all of these difficulties. If we can recognize that such disturbances simply form a part of the drama and the illusion of this temporary world and involve the challenges that we must face in order to return back to the spiritual kingdom, we will not feel overly disturbed. This will give us the necessary strength and enthusiasm to transcend the enemies of the mind. Otherwise, we will just overwhelm our minds and weaken our bodies by the excessive adrenaline in the system, which will also interfere with our spiritual absorption.

We want to do that which will enhance our ability to more easily embrace our spiritual life. Sometimes we just have to relax the muscles, engage in deeper breathing, and oxygenate the blood through laughter. We can have the biggest laugh by laughing at ourselves sometimes. We can think, "I really made a big mistake but now I can move away from the past. It was so foolish of me to accept these issues as my real and full identity. Actually, for many lifetimes I have acted quite foolishly so now I should move through these issues very quickly while understanding the insignificance of this lifetime in the total scheme of reality." When we return to the spiritual world, we will not have any of these interferences that inhibit the joy and beauty of spiritual life.

Although we have to struggle in different ways, we do not want to forget the joys of spiritual life. We can remind ourselves of that joy just by reflecting more on the Lord's mercy and pastimes. We included a few of the different pastimes in order to reflect on the nature of some of the eternal pastimes in the spiritual world according to ancient Vedic wisdom. In this way, we can increasingly prepare ourselves to return back home, especially by beginning to act like the residents in our home. As you read the various pastimes in the sacred scriptures, just pay more attention to what you read because you will notice the amazing interactions between the Supreme Lord and His devotees. Since we can never actually separate ourselves from the spiritual realities, we can develop that kind of richness simply by codifying the world differently. We want to help each other codify things in a way that energize us. It means that sometimes we have to help each other see the illusions and our faults and weaknesses but also remind each other of our ultimate purity. We are ultimately engaged in spiritual processes so that we can recognize our eternal identity. We can better recognize that reality when we stop accepting these temporary involvements and associations as ourselves. There are really no such things as mundane anxiety, fear, anger, grief, and depression. They are not tangible. They are manufactured illusions, which are created from unhealthy codifications and perceptions. We have created them. We have hosted them so now we can laugh as we reject their existence and as we see them as perverted reflections and indications of true emotions connected with the Godhead.

Epilogue

Kenneth "Khensu" Carter, M.D.

The psychosomatic socialization institution that puts the human brain-body-mind to sleep, and inhibits the evolving spiritual metamorphosis journey of the soul is the most insidious mental health illness of our times. The notion that man is a spiritual and psychological being is a popular platitude. We rarely grasp its implications. We don't ordinarily think for example of spirit profoundly affecting the mind or mind affecting the body. Nor do we think of the evolutionary processes we find in the physical world also occurring in the mind. And we don't ordinarily imagine the "reality" of our mind and its emotions as a scene of constant, sophisticated, spiritual warfare. Mind produces defenses in response to perceived attacks and mind develops resistance. If we were to comprehend the real meaning of psychological evolution, then we would envision a world in which every emotion and thought we have is changing at every instant in response to every other emotion or thought that we or someone else may have.

Whole patterns of feeling and thinking are rising and falling, shifting and changing. This restless and perpetual change, as inexorable and unstoppable as the waves and tides, implies a world in which all human actions necessarily have uncertain effects. The total system we call "mind" is so complicated that we can't know in advance the consequences of anything that we do. That's why even our most enlightened past efforts have yielded undesirable results, either because we did not understand enough, or because our ever-changing "state of mind" responded in unexpected ways.

From this standpoint, the system of mental health treatment in the western world is as discouraging as mental health neglect. Anyone who is willing to argue, for example, that the "psychological" approach of treating patients with talk therapy is any less damaging than the "biological" approach of treating patients with drug therapy ignores the fact that both approaches have been carried out with utter conviction and both have altered patients minds irrevocably to the exclusion of any substantive consideration of psychological evolution or spiritual capacity. Both provide ample evidence of the dogged egotism that is a hallmark of human interaction intrapsychically and with each other.

The fact that mind responds unpredictably to our actions is not an argument for inaction. It is however a powerful argument for caution and for adopting a tentative attitude toward all we believe and all we do. If we but recognize that modern (biomechanical) medicine is barely a hundred years old and its psychological theories even less than that, we will not be surprised by its inadequacies. If we recognize this, we will be bold and persistent in our responsibility to ask and investigate "what are we **really** doing?"

Unfortunately, our society has demonstrated a striking lack of caution in the past. It's hard to imagine that we will behave differently in the future. We think we know what we are doing. We seem "hardwired" to think so. We never seem to acknowledge that we have been wrong in the past and so might be wrong in the future. Instead, each generation writes off earlier errors as bad thinking by less able minds and then confidently embarks on fresh errors of its own.

As a species, modern medicine and the western tradition generally view humans as uniquely self-aware, yet self-delusion may be a more significant characteristic of our kind. Collectively and individually, our self-deluded psychological state has collided with our growing technological power in the physical world. In the absence of a counterbalancing spiritual technology, we truly threaten the existence of the entire world. Answers to this dilemma are not coming from the mainstream of mental health, which, pathologically enthralled with the science of pathology can offer no means to escape into health. The ancient sciences of spiritual technology are increasingly usurping the mainstream. This process is slow, incomplete, piecemeal, and reluctant as the "ivory tower" responds to the growing hunger within patients for more than their biomechanical and psychological paradigms can provide.

We have had ample experience with the problems of mental health, biological psychiatry, and the accompanying psychological theories. What all three have in common is the absence of a unifying spiritual technology that embraces biological, psychological, social, and individual dimensions. We have lived for some years with the "biopsychosocial" model of contemporary psychiatry as an abstract ideal with no unifying praxis. It is a great idea, but in actual practice this tri-partite concept is more akin to three individual units working in parallel than an integrated cohesive whole working together.

Antibiotic interventions, unbridled and without appropriate context, have contributed to the resistance and evolutionary acceleration of the very organisms we sought to eradicate. Similarly, our mental health interventions often cause injury and harm despite even the best intentions. Psychoactive drugs have not proven to be golden bullets or panaceas for mental illness (e.g., depression, anxiety, psychosis) and may contribute to the very illnesses they seek to cure. Persons suffering the brunt of social affront continue to be routed through institutions of social control without ever addressing root causes and problems. From the mistakes in the 1860's of labeling runaway slaves with a form of mania, to the mistakes in the 1960's in labeling the mothers of schizophrenic patients "schizophrenogenic", to the use of the popular diagnosis ADD today as 'wastebasket diagnosis' for children of various biological, psychological, and social situations, it is difficult to argue that mental health labels have rendered, overall, any less harm than good.

Recent findings in psychosomatic medicine and the growth of alternative medicine have led many to rethink old assumptions. Body/mind, spirit/matter, me/you, they/we are not as separate as once imagined. Studies document that our patients with characteristics of spirituality—i.e., spiritual beliefs and practices—generally have better outcomes. Researchers admonish, however, that religiosity is not the same as spirituality. Spirituality helps to improve medical outcomes; religiosity does not. Although the concept of spiritual technology is new to most practitioners and patients, the potential impact for both is enormous.

We cannot be casual about these issues in the future as we have been in the past. The quest to alleviate suffering, especially our own and that of our own making, is one that has no equal. The cause of "Physician Heal Thyself" must begin with the enemies of our own minds and those whom we most directly touch. Negative thoughts and emotions can separate us from others and from our own peace and happiness. The well-spring of ancient wisdom is abundantly rich with advice and praxis to help us heal modern-day dilemmas.

His Holiness Bhakti Tirtha Swami (Swami Krishnapada) shares with us insights in spiritual technology from ancient sources that are in many ways the most radical and scientifically advanced lifestyle and thought systems available to us. He espouses the application of a mental health approach based on spiritual realities that integrate individual and social healing themes across the range of human experience and opportunity.

Those of us who feel the need must take our own first steps to help shape the emergence of spirit-based practices for the present and the future. That is the subject of this book. His Holiness, a jewel in the unbroken chain of ancestral wisdom, has given us wonderful technologies to help us address the whole person. This book is a wake-up call for a more comprehensive approach to healing the individual, institutions, and the global community.

Kenneth "Khensu" Carter, M.D., M.P.H., Dipl. Ac. (Master of Public Health, Board Certified in Psychiatry and Acupuncture)

266 Spiritual Warrior IV

Notes

[1] Prabhupada, *The Journey of Self-Discovery*, 120-121.

[2] All purports from the *Bhagavad-gita*, *Srimad-Bhagavatam*, and *Sri Caitanya-caritamrta* are quoted from A. C. Bhaktivedanta Swami Prabhupada's translations and commentaries on these Vedic scriptures. See full citations in the Bibliography.

[3] Prabhupada, *Krsna Consciousness: Topmost Yoga System*, 99.

[4] Prabhupada, *The Path of Perfection*, 55.

[5] De Becker, *Fear Less*, 25.

[6] Richard E. Behrman, M.D., ed., "Sexual Abuse of Children," *The Future of Children* 4, no. 2 (Summer/Fall 1994), 10.

[7] Foundation for Inner Peace, *A Course in Miracles*.

[8] Chris Raymond, "Distrust, Rage May Be 'Toxic Core' That Puts 'Type A' Person at Risk,' *Journal of the American Medical Association* 261, no. 6 (1989): 813.

[9] A.C. Bhaktivedanta Swami Prabhupada letter to Gajendra, 27 January 1970, *Srila Prabhupada Siksamrta* (Los Angeles: Bhaktivedanta Book Trust, 1992), 3: 1949.

[10] A.C. Bhaktivedanta Swami Prabhupada, *The Nectar of Instruction*, 5.

[11] A.C. Bhaktivedanta Swami Prabhupada, "Lectures and Classes, *Srimad-Bhagavatam* 6.1.15—New York, August 1, 1971," *The Bhaktivedanta VedaBase* Ver. 4.11, CD-ROM, (The Bhaktivedanta Archives, 1998).

[12] Ibid., "Lectures and Classes, Purports to Songs, Purport to *Gaura Pahu*-Los Angeles, January 10, 1969."

[13] World Health Organization, *The World Health Report 2001: Mental Health: New Understanding, New Hope* (Geneva, 2001).

[14] Quoted by Jayapataka Maharaja.

[15] See the two volume work edited by Robert Ader, David L. Felten, and Nicholas Cohen, *Psychoneuroimmunology*, 3rd ed. (San Diego: Academic Press, 2001).

[16] David G. Myers, *Psychology* 6th ed. (New York: Worth Publishers, 2001).

[17] Margaret A. Shugart, M.D. and Elda M. Lopez, M.D., "Depression in Children and Adolescents," *Postgraduate Medicine* 112, no. 3 (September 2002): 54-55.

[18] C. Smith, et al., *Key Topics in Psychiatry*, (Oxford: BIOS Scientific Publishers Limited, 1996), 203-205.

[19] Hara Estroff Marano, "The Depression Suite," *Psychology Today*, (May/June 2003): 60.

[20] Ibid., 62

[21] Ibid., 64.

[22] Saint John of the Cross, *Dark Night of the Soul.*

[23] World Health Organization, Women's Health and Development, *Violence Against Women: A Priority Health Issue* (Geneva, 1997).

[24] World Health Organization, *World Health Day: Active Aging Makes the Difference* (Geneva, 1999).

[25] Thakur Bhakti Vinode, *Shri Chaitanya Shikshamritam*, 65-69.

[26] Prabhupada Saraswati Thakura, *The Life and Teachings of Bhaktisiddhanta Saraswati*, 98.

[27] Annemieke Mol Lous et al., "Depression markers in young children's play: a comparison between depressed and nondepressed 3-to-6-year-olds in various play situation," *Journal of Child Psychology and Psychiatry* 43, no. 8 (2002): 1029-1038.

[28] Thakur Bhakti Vinode, *Shri Chaitanya Shikshamritam*, 65-69.

[29] Peter A. Boxer, Carol Burnett, and Naomi Swanson, "Suicide and Occupation: A Review of the Literature," *JOEM* 37, no. 4 (April 1995), 446.

[30] Ruth E. Levine and Stephen G. Bryant, "The Depressed Physician: A Different Kind of Impairment," *Hospital Physician* (February, 2000), 86.

[31] Sarah Knox, Stephen G. Virginia, and John P. Lombardo, "Depression and Anxiety in Roman Catholic Secular Clergy," *Pastoral Psychology* 50, no. 5 (2002): 345-358.

[32] Bill W., *Alcoholics Anonymous: The Story of How Many Thousands of Men and Women Have Recovered from Alcoholism*, 3rd ed. (New York: Alcoholics Anonymous World Services, 1986), 59-60.

[33] The following two books can further your interest in the subject: John E. Mack, *Abduction: Human Encounters with Aliens*, (New York: rev. ed. Ballantine Books, 1995); Whitley Strieber, *Communion: A True Story*, (New York: Beech Tree Books, 1987).

[34] William F. Fry, "The Biology of Humor," *Humor: International Journal of Humor Research* 7, no. 2 (1994): 111-112.

[35] Ibid., 114-116.

[36] United Nations Office for Drug Control and Crime Prevention, *World Drug Report 2000* (New York: Oxford University Press, 2000).

[37] John Fetto, "A Royal Flush," *American Demographics*, (September 2002): 72.

[38] Prabhupada, *The Nectar of Devotion*, 361-364.

Glossary

Acarya: A spiritual master who teaches by his own example, and who sets the proper religious example for all human beings.

Adhibhautika: Misery caused by other living beings.

Adhidaivika: Misery or natural disturbances caused by the demigods.

Adhyatmika: Miseries arising from one's own body and mind.

Ahankara: False ego, by which the soul misidentifies with the material body.

Anartha: Unwanted material desires in the heart that pollute one's consciousness, such as pride, hate, envy, lust, greed, anger, and desires for distinction, adoration, wealth, etc.

Asrama: The four spiritual orders according to the Vedic social system: *brahmacarya* (student life), *grhastha* (householder life), *vanaprastha* (retirement), and *sannyasa* (renunciation).

Astanga-yoga: The eightfold system of mystic *yoga*, propounded by Patanjali, meant for realizing the presence of Paramatma, the Lord in the heart.

Avatara: Literally means "one who descends." A partially or fully empowered incarnation of the Lord who descends from the spiritual sky to the material universe with a particular mission described in the scriptures.

Bhakti-lata-bija: The seed of the creeper of devotional service.

Bhakti-yoga: The system of cultivation of *bhakti*, or pure devotional service, which is untinged by sense gratification or philosophical speculation.

Bhakti: Devotional service to the Supreme Lord.

Bhaya: Fear.

Brahmana: A member of the most intelligent class of men, according to the four Vedic occupational divisions of society.

Deva: A demigod or saintly person.

Dharma: Religious principles; one's natural occupation.

Dhira: One who is undisturbed by the material energy in all circumstances.

Drdha-vrata: Firm determination.

Guru: Spiritual master.

Hatha-yoga: The practice of postures and breathing exercises for achieving purification and sense control.

Hladini-sakti: The pleasure potency of God.

Jnana: The path of empirical knowledge, culminating in attainment of impersonal liberation (*sayujya-mukti*).

Jnana-yoga: The path of spiritual realization through a speculative philosophical search for truth.

Jnani: A transcendentalist who attempts to obtain impersonal liberation as a result of empirical knowledge.

Kama: Lust.

Karma: The law of material cause and effect.

Karma-yoga: The process of mundane religious sacrifice as recommended in the *karma-kanda* sections of the Vedas.

Karmi: A fruitive worker who attempts to enjoy heavenly bliss through the process of *karma-yoga*.

Krodha: Anger.

Ksatriya: The martial-spirited, administrative class of Vedic society who protect society from danger.

Lobha: Greed.

Mada: Madness.

Maha-tattva: The total material energy.

Mantra: A pure sound vibration that delivers the mind from its material inclinations and illusions when repeated over and over. A transcendental sound or Vedic hymn, prayer, or chant.

Martya-loka: The "world of death," the earth.

Matsarya: Envy.

Maya: The external energy of the Supreme Lord, which covers the conditioned soul and does not allow him to understand the Supreme Personality of Godhead.

Moha: Bewilderment or illusion.

Pandita: A learned Vedic scholar whose knowledge is based on scripture.

Paramatma: The Supersoul, the localized aspect of Visnu expansion of the Supreme Lord residing in the heart of each embodied living entity and pervading all of material nature.

Prabhu: Master.

Prema: Love; pure and unbreakable love of God.

Raksasa: A class of ungodly people always opposed to God's will. They are generally man-eaters and have grotesque forms.

Rsi: A sage who performs austerities.

Ruci: Liking, taste.

Sac-cid-ananda-vigraha: The Lord's transcendental form, which is eternal and full of knowledge and bliss.

Sadhana: Systematic practices aimed at spiritual perfection, especially Deity worship and chanting the holy name of the Lord.

Sadhana-bhakti: There are nine limbs to the practice of *sadhana-bhakti*: hearing, chanting, remembering, serving, Deity worship, offering everything, friendship, and surrendering everything.

Sadhu: A saintly person.

Sakti: Spiritual energy.

Sankirtana: The congregational chanting of the holy name, fame, and pastimes of the Lord.

Sastra: Revealed scripture; Vedic literature.

Siddhanta: Conclusion.

Sisya: Disciple.

Vijnana: The practical realization of spiritual knowledge.

Yogi: A transcendentalist who practices one of the many authorized forms of *yoga*, or processes of spiritual purification.

Bibliography

Ader, Robert; David L. Felten; and Nicholas Cohen. *Psychoneuroimmunology.* 2 vols. San Diego: Academic Press, 2001.

Carnegie, Dale. *How to Stop Worrying and Start Living.* New York: Pocket Books, 1984.

Carter, Les and Minirth, Frank M.D. *The Choosing to Forgive Workbook.* Nashville: Thomas Nelson Publishers, 1997.

De Becker, Gavin. *Fear Less: Real Truth About Risk, Safety, and Security in a Time of Terrorism.* Boston: Little Brown and Co., 2002.

DeFoore, Bill. *Anger: Deal With It, Heal With It, Stop It From Killing You.* Deerfield Beach, Florida: Health Communications, Inc., 1991.

Foundation for Inner Peace. *A Course in Miracles*: Combined Volume. 2nd ed. Newly Rev. New York: Viking, 1996.

John of the Cross, Saint. *Dark Night of the Soul*. Translated by Mirabai Starr. New York: Riverhead Books, 2002.

Mack, John E. *Abduction: Human Encounters with Aliens*. Rev. ed. New York: Ballantine Books, 1995.

McKay, Matthew; Rogers, Peter D.; and McKay, Judith R.N. *When Anger Hurts: Quieting the Storm Within*. Oakland, CA: New Harbinger Publications, Inc., 1989.

Prabhupada, A. C. Bhaktivedanta Swami. *Bhagavad-gita As It Is*. Los Angeles: Bhaktivedanta Book Trust, 1983.

———. *The Bhaktivedanta VedaBase* Ver. 4.11. CD-ROM. The Bhaktivedanta Archives, 1998.

———. *The Journey of Self-Discovery*. Los Angeles: Bhaktivedanta Book Trust, 1990.

———. *Srimad-Bhagavatam*. 18 vols. Los Angeles: Bhaktivedanta Book Trust, 1987.

———. *Sri Caitanya-caritamrta*. 9 vols. Los Angeles: Bhaktivedanta Book Trust, 1996.

———. *Krsna Consciousness: Topmost Yoga System*. [New York/ Los Angeles]: Bhaktivedanta Book Trust, 1972.

———. *The Nectar of Devotion*. Los Angeles: Bhaktivedanta Book Trust, 1982.

———. *The Nectar of Instruction*. New York: Bhaktivedanta Book Trust, 1975.

Prabhupada Saraswati Thakura, *The Life and Teachings of Bhaktisiddhanta Saraswati*. Oregon: Mandala Publishing Group, 1997.

Safer, Jeanne. *Forgiving and Not Forgiving: A New Approach to Resolving Intimate Betrayal*. New York: Avon Books, 1999.

Strieber, Whitley. *Communion: A True Story*. New York: Beech Tree Books, 1987.

Thakur, Bhakti Vinode. *Shri Caitanya Shikshamritam*. Translated by Shri Bijoy Krishna Rarhi. Chennai: Shri Gaudiya Math, n.d.

W., Bill. *Alcoholics Anonymous: The Story of How Many Thousands of Men and Women Have Recovered from Alcoholism*, 3rd ed. New York: Alcoholics Anonymous World Services, 1986.

Index

About the Author

Bhakti-Tirtha Swami Krishnapada was born John E. Favors in a pious, God-fearing family. As a child evangelist he appeared regularly on television. As a young man he was a leader in Dr. Martin Luther King, Jr.'s civil rights movement. At Princeton University he became president of the student council and also served as chairman of the Third World Coalition. Although his main degree is in psychology, he has received accolades in many other fields, including politics, African studies, and international law.

Bhakti-Tirtha Swami's books are used as reference texts in universities and leadership organizations throughout the world. Many of his books have been printed in English, German, French, Spanish, Portuguese, Macedonian, Croatian, Russian, Hebrew, Slovenian, Balinese and Italian.

His Holiness has served as Assistant Coordinator for penal reform programs in the State of New Jersey, Office of the Public

Defender, and as a director of several drug abuse clinics in the United States. In addition, he has been a special consultant for Educational Testing Services in the U.S.A. and has managed campaigns for politicians. Bhakti-Tirtha Swami gained international recognition as a representative of the Bhaktivedanta Book Trust, particularly for his outstanding work with scholars in the former communist countries of Eastern Europe.

Bhakti-Tirtha Swami directly oversees projects in the United States (particularly Washington D.C., Potomac, Maryland, Detroit, Pennsylvania, West Virginia), West Africa, South Africa, Switzerland, France, Croatia and Bosnia. He also serves as the director of the American Federation of Vaisnava Colleges and Schools.

In the United States, Bhakti-Tirtha Swami is the founder and director of the Institute for Applied Spiritual Technology, director of the International Committee for Urban Spiritual Development and one of the international coordinators of the Seventh Pan African Congress. Reflecting his wide range of interests, he is also a member of the Institute for Noetic Sciences, the Center for Defense Information, the United Nations Association for America, the National Peace Institute Foundation, the World Future Society and the Global Forum of Spiritual and Parliamentary Leaders.

A specialist in international relations and conflict resolution, Bhakti-Tirtha Swami constantly travels around the world and has become a spiritual consultant to many high-ranking members of the United Nations, to various celebrities and to several chiefs, kings and high court justices. In 1990 His Holiness was coronated as a high chief in Warri, Nigeria in recognition of his outstanding work in Africa and the world. In recent years, he has met several times with then-President Nelson Mandela of South Africa to share visions and strategies for world peace.

In addition to encouraging self-sufficiency through the development of schools, clinics, farm projects and cottage industries, Bhakti-Tirtha Swami conducts seminars and workshops on principle centered leadership, spiritual development, interpersonal relationships, stress and time management and other pertinent topics. He is also widely acknowledged as a viable participant in the resolution of global conflict.

Leadership for an Age of Higher Consciousness I

Administration from a Metaphysical Perspective

by B.T. Swami
(Swami Krishnapada)

$23.00 hardbound ISBN #1-885414-02-1
$14.95 softbound ISBN #1-885414-05-6
320 pages, 2nd edition

"An example in the truest sense of global principle-centered leadership, Swami Krishnapada manages to take consciousness-raising to its highest platform of self-realized actuality in humanizing the workplace. My experience in working with all of the nations of the world convinces me that such a book is the corporate leadership guide for the coming millennium."

The Honorable Pierre Adossama
Director, Labor Relations (Retired)
International Labor Organization
United Nations

The Leader In You

Leadership in any capacity has taken on such awesome proportions that even the best leaders must find innovative and creative ways to deal with today's complex situations. *Leadership for an Age of Higher Consciousness: Administration from a Metaphysical Perspective* is a ground breaking self-help manual written for those who seek to develop a more penetrating perspective and greater effectiveness in the leadership process. This book is relevant for heads of government, organizations and families, and for anyone seeking greater insight into self-leadership.

Leadership for an Age of Higher Consciousness II

Ancient Wisdom For Modern Times

by B.T. Swami
(Swami Krishnapada)

$23.00 hardbound ISBN #1-885414-11-0
$14.95 softbound ISBN #1-885414-12-9
209 pages, 1st edition

"Good leadership is not just a matter of making things happen; it is a matter of making essential things happen, making important and productive things happen, and helping people feel good about what is happening. Leaders need to have a vision, but they also need to know how to convince others that their vision can manifest, and how to empower them to participate in the mission of bringing the vision about."

—*Excerpt from Leadership for an Age of Higher Consciousness, Vol. 2*

Become An Authentic Leader

In this sequel to his internationally acclaimed *Leadership for an Age of Higher Consciousness: Administration from a Metaphysical Perspective*, His Holiness Bhakti-Tirtha Swami Krishnapada explores the greatness of two famous leaders from the Vedic tradition of ancient India. Addressing the leader within each of us, B.T. Swami shows us that the greatest leaders see themselves as servants first, they place integrity and character before personal gain, and they know how to tap into the help that is available from both the earthly and spiritual realms. True servant leaders are animated visionaries who cultivate divine power to transform diverse individuals with scattered goals into communities with a unified, sacred mission.

Spiritual Warrior I

Uncovering Spiritual Truths
in Psychic Phenomena

by B.T. Swami
(Swami Krishnapada)

$12.95 softbound ISBN #1-885414-01-3
200 pages, 2nd edition

"As we rapidly approach the new millennium, more and more people are searching for spiritual answers to the meaning and purpose of life. The search, of course, begins with Self, and Swami Krishnapada's book, *Spiritual Warrior*, provides a practical companion for the journey of the initiate. I am honored to recommend it."

Gordon-Michael Scallion
Futurist; Editor,
Earth Changes Report
Matrix Institute, Inc.

Ancient Mysteries Revealed!

Get ready for a roller-coaster ride into the intriguing realm of ancient mysteries! It is rare to find the subjects in this book handled in such a piercing and straightforward way. *Spiritual Warrior: Uncovering Spiritual Truths in Psychic Phenomena* focuses on the spiritual essence of many topics that have bewildered scholars and scientists for generations, such as extraterrestrials, the pyramids and psychic intrusion. A fresh perspective is revealed, inviting the reader to expand the boundaries of the mind and experience a true and lasting connection with the inner self.

The Beggar II

Crying Out for the Mercy

Commune with the Lord

by B.T. Swami
(Swami Krishnapada)

$11.95 softbound ISBN #1-885414-04-8
184 pages

This deeply inspirational offering to the Lord and His devotees is Bhakti-Tirtha Swami's wonderful follow-up book to *The Beggar I: Meditations and Prayers on the Supreme Lord.* You'll love this all new collection of prayers, meditations and essays, as they make you cry, laugh, and most of all, commune with that innermost part of you that's crying out for the mercy. This book is a must read, so order yours now, and get ready for the Lord's mercy!

"Immediately I felt the weight of my deficiencies, and realized how polluted my consciousness had become. The voice continued speaking, giving me a welcome distraction.

'Despite your many deficiencies, I have been drawn to you by the intensity of your greed and desperation for transcendence. In fact, I have been sanctioned by higher authority to reveal your shortcomings to you. I therefore beg you to listen closely, for this is a rare opportunity that may not come again for many lifetimes.'

I braced myself for a rude awakening..." —*excerpts from The Beggar II*

B.T. SWAMI
False Ego: The Greatest Enemy of the Spiritual Leader

The Beggar III

False Ego: The Greatest Enemy of the Spiritual Leader

Release Your True Self

"Bhakti-Tirtha Swami's books are all written to facilitate us in keeping our highest Self in charge of our lives as we move toward our greatest potential and highest good. *The Beggar III* is his latest contribution to helping us do the often-difficult inner work of understanding that our life force is our God force. Typical of all true leaders, he teaches by loving, living example."

John T. Chissell, M.D.
Author: *Pyramids of Power*

by B.T. Swami
(Swami Krishnapada)

$12.95 softbound ISBN #1-885414-10-2
215 pages

"...Selflessness is the ingredient most lacking in today's world, because people misunderstand the purpose and principle behind this wonderful science. Genuine selflessness is not thinking less of yourself, but thinking of yourself less.

"My mentor continued: 'Selflessness doesn't mean to give up pursuing adventurous goals, but rather to attach ourselves to transcendental goals. Actual selflessness means we must genuinely access humility and submissiveness. This can be very scary, because we normally identify humility and submissiveness with low self-esteem.'"

—*excerpts from The Beggar III*

Order on the web at **www.ifast.net**

Reflections on Sacred Teachings

Volume One: Sri Siksastaka

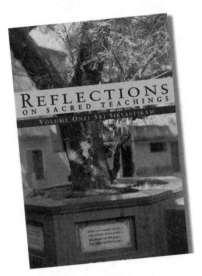

by B.T. Swami
(Swami Krishnapada)

$14.95, softbound ISBN #1-885414-13-7
260 pages

"O Govinda! Feeling Your separation, I am considering a moment to be like twelve years or more. Tears are flowing from my eyes like torrents of rain and I am feeling all vacant in the world in Your absence."

Explore Timeless Wisdom

"Lord Caitanya Mahaprabhu instructed His disciples to write books on the science of Krishna, a task which those who follow Him have continued to carry out down to the present day. The elaborations and expositions on the philosophy taught by Lord Caitanya are in fact most voluminous, exacting and consistent due to the system of disciplic succession. Although Lord Caitanya was widely renowned as a scholar in His youth, He left only eight verses, called *Siksastaka*. These eight verses clearly reveal His mission and precepts."

– A.C. Bhaktivedanta Swami Prabhupada

Nearly five hundred years after Lord Caitanya Mahaprabhu walked among us, the *Sri Siksastaka* verses continue to lead all Vaisnavas ever deeper into the science and experience of pure, spontaneous and enveloping love of God.

His Holiness Bhakti-Tirtha Swami explores these verses from a contemporary perspective and helps modern devotees derive strength and realization from this timeless message, while reminding us of the important role we must play in carrying Lord Caitanya's legacy to future generations.

Order on the web at **www.ifast.net**

Reflections on Sacred Teachings

Volume Two: Madhurya-Kadambini

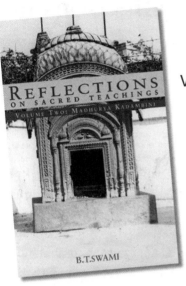

by B.T. Swami
(Swami Krishnapada)

$14.95, softbound ISBN #1-885414-14-5
244 pages

The Sweetness of Devotion

The Bhakti Trilogy is one of the great works of Visvanatha Cakravarti and his first presentation is the *Madhurya-Kadambini*. The word *kadambini* means a long bank of clouds that are showering *madhurya*, the sweetness of devotion. These clouds manifest over the environment to shower the *madhurya* and extinguish the blazing forest fire of material attraction and attachments. His Holiness Bhakti-Tirtha Swami explores these verses as a way of reminding the reader how such mentors and their teachings, although ancient, are as relevant now as they were in the past. Let the *madhurya*, the sweetness of devotion, shower us all as we take shelter of Srila Visvanatha Cakravarti Thakura's unlimited mercy.

"Srila Visvanatha Cakravarti has given us a detailed analysis of the obstructions to our individual and collective devotional service. He has also given us a sublime outline of the stages of progress up to *prema*. Now the challenge is before each of us to fully use what he has given us. How blessed we all are to receive this opportunity through the blueprints given by such great *acaryas*, to facilitate us in returning back to the realm of pure, enchanting, enduring and animated love."

Order on the web at **www.ifast.net**

Reflections on Sacred Teachings

Volume Three: Harinama Cintamani

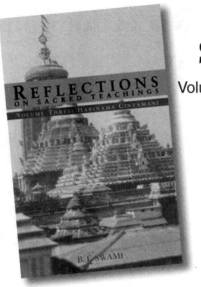

The Holy Name Is The Key

by B.T. Swami
(Swami Krishnapada)

$14.95, softbound ISBN #1-885414-15-3
308 pages

"In previous ages, a person could reach perfection through meditation, temple worship or *yajnas* but in Kali-yuga, we cannot even perform one of the nine-fold activities nicely. Although just one of these nine activities can result in full love of Godhead, we engage in all nine and still have problems. Fortunately Srila Haridasa reveals the holy name as a source of hope in spite of the constant challenges in this Kali-yuga."

—*excerpts from Harinama Cintamani*

"*Sri Harinama Cintamani* is the extraordinary conversation between the Supreme Lord Sri Caitanya Mahaprabhu and His devotee Srila Haridasa Thakura on the potency and efficacy of the holy name. His Holiness Bhakti-Tirtha Swami, a devout spiritual teacher in the Vaisnava line, leads us through the *Sri Harinama Cintamani* step-by-step, and enables us to hold onto the key of the holy name, unlocking the mysteries of our own pure and effulgent qualities. Srila Haridasa explains that the holy name will reach out—in spite of all the barriers and formalities—to the person who grabs and holds onto it.

Order on the web at **www.ifast.net**

Order Form

Item	Quant	Costs	Item	Quant	Costs
Leadership for an Age of Higher Consciousness, Vol. 1	hard $23.00 x ___ = $ _____ soft $14.95 x ___ = $ _____		The Beggar, Vol. 2	soft $11.95 x ___ = $ _____	
Leadership for an Age of Higher Consciousness, Vol. 2	hard $23.00 x ___ = $ _____ soft $14.95 x ___ = $ _____		The Beggar, Vol. 3	soft $12.95 x ___ = $ _____	
Spiritual Warrior, Vol. 1	soft $12.95 x ___ = $ _____		Reflections on Sacred Teachings, Vol. 1	soft $14.95 x ___ = $ _____	
Spiritual Warrior, Vol. 2	hard $12.95 x ___ = $ _____ soft $20.00 x ___ = $ _____		Reflections on Sacred Teachings, Vol. 2	soft $14.95 x ___ = $ _____	
Spiritual Warrior, Vol. 2 audio tapes and CDs	10 tapes $45.00 x ___ = $ _____ 9 CDs $60.00 x ___ = $ _____		Reflections on Sacred Teachings, Vol. 3	soft $14.95 x ___ = $ _____	
Spiritual Warrior, Vol. 3	hard $23.00 x ___ = $ _____ soft $14.95 x ___ = $ _____				
Spiritual Warrior, Vol. 4	soft $14.95 x ___ = $ _____				
Spiritual Warrior, Vol. 5	soft $14.95 x ___ = $ _____				
The Beggar, Vol. 1	soft $11.95 x ___ = $ _____				
The Beggar, Vol. 1 audio tapes	6 tapes $28.00 x ___ = $ _____				

Subtotal		
Shipping & Handling		
Total		

○ I'd like more information on other books, CDs, audiotapes and videotapes from HNP.

Name: _____

Address: _____

City: _____ State: _____ Zip: _____

Daytime Phone: _____ Evening Phone: _____

Email Address: _____

Shipping and handling: **USA:** $5.00 for first book and $1.75 for each additional book. Air mail per book (USA only): $5.00. **Outside of the USA:** $8.00 for first book and $4.00 for each additional book. Surface shipping may take 3-4 weeks. Foreign orders: please allow 6-8 weeks for delivery.

Internet: www.ifast.net/hnp
Mail: Hari-Nama Press, PO Box 76451, Washington DC 20013